THE

OVERWHELMING

QUESTION

BALACHANDRA RAJAN

The Overwhelming Question

A STUDY OF

THE POETRY OF

T.S. ELIOT

UNIVERSITY OF TORONTO PRESS

TORONTO AND BUFFALO

© University of Toronto Press 1976
Toronto and Buffalo
Printed in Canada

Library of Congress Cataloging in Publication Data

Rajan, Balachandra.
   The overwhelming question.

   Bibliography: p.
   Includes index.
   1. Eliot, Thomas Stearns, 1888-1965 – Criticism and
interpretation. I. Title.
PS3509.L43Z818   821'.9'12   75-32519
ISBN 0-8020-2187-5

Contents

Foreword

This book is one of three explorations of differing patterns of wholeness in major writers. The first exploration was of Yeats's work and was published in 1965. In *The Lofty Rhyme*, published in 1970, I attempted to define and to elaborate the wholeness of Milton's accomplishment. Therefore while the present book can, I hope, stand by itself, it also has a place within a larger structure.

I had originally intended this book to be the first of the three. It might have been written in 1957 when the Bollingen Foundation generously gave me an award for the writing of a book on Eliot. At that time I was a member of the Indian Foreign Service and was unable to secure the leave of absence needed to begin work on the book. Several years later when I had returned to academic life, the Foundation learned of this and by offering to renew the award, reaffirmed its confidence in the project in a manner for which I could not but be grateful. I was then too preoccupied with my second book on Milton to be able to take advantage of the Foundation's considerateness. This book is a tardy but I hope not unfitting response to the Foundation's persisting belief that I was capable of writing something that mattered on Eliot.

The opportunity to complete this book was made available through a sabbatical year given me by the University of Western Ontario and a Leave Fellowship awarded by the Canada Council. I am grateful to have had the time for thought and hope the thought has profited from the time.

The first chapter of this book originally appeared in *The Sewanee Review* 74 (Winter 1966). Copyright 1966 by the University of the South. Reprinted by permission of the editor. The issue, edited by Allen Tate, was republished in book form by Chatto and Windus under the title *T.S. Eliot: The Man and His Work*. The second chapter first appeared in *The Waste Land in Different Voices*, edited by David Moody and published by Edward Arnold. It is reprinted by permission of Edward Arnold. My thanks are also due to Mrs Betty Ann Muill for finding time in the midst of other duties for the prompt and willing typing of these pages and to Barbara Macdonald for typing the index.

This book has been published with the help of grants from the Humanities Research Council of Canada, using funds provided by the Canada Council, and the Publications Fund of the University of Toronto Press.

BR

THE

OVERWHELMING

QUESTION

CHAPTER ONE

The Overwhelming Question

To read 'Tradition and the Individual Talent' today is to become aware of its distinguished obsolescence. The essay takes its place among those monuments, the ideal order of which it once sought to alter by the injection of the radically new. Literary judgement moves onward though not necessarily forward; and the expanding worlds of the collective and the anonymous, the growth of mass communications and the increasing difficulty of communicating the authentic, have given to words like 'personality' and 'identity' a rallying power they once did not possess. The struggle to achieve definition without exterior compromise is now a condition of the creative conscience. In such circumstances, it becomes almost necessary to remind ourselves that the famous words which follow were the clarion call of criticism forty years ago.

> Poetry is not a turning loose of emotion, but an escape from emotion; it is not the expression of personality, but an escape from personality. But, of course, only those who have personality and emotions know what it means to want to escape from these things.[1]

One test of a critic is his power to repent. As the times changed, Eliot changed cautiously with them. Fifteen years later he had carried his flight from personality sufficiently far to look detachedly over his shoulder at whatever was pursuing him.

> The whole of Shakespeare's work is *one* poem; and it is the poetry of it in this sense, not the poetry of isolated lines and passages or the poetry of the single figures which he created, that matters most. A man might, hypothetically, compose any number of fine passages or even of whole poems which would each give satisfaction, and yet not be a great poet, unless we felt them to be united by one significant, consistent, and developing personality.[2]

The juxtaposition is not offered as a lesson in historical irony. To change one's mind, as has been suggested, is an indication that one's mind is alive. With Eliot the change is important not only because it is not unreasonable, but because of the weight it assumes in his later critical doctrine. A year prior to the essay on John Ford from which the passage above is quoted, Eliot had expressed a similar view on Herbert: 'Throughout there is brain work, and a very high level of intensity: his poetry is definitely an œuvre to be studied entire.'[3] In 1939, in considering Yeats's growth as a poet, Eliot found the merit of the later poetry to lie in the fuller expression of personality within it.[4] In 1944, the test of wholeness was applied to Milton:

> The important difference is whether a knowledge of the whole, or at least of a very large part, of a poet's work, makes one enjoy more, because it makes one understand better, any one of his poems. That implies a significant unity in his whole work. One can't put this increased understanding altogether into words: I could not say just why I think I understand *Comus* better for having read *Paradise Lost*, or *Paradise Lost* better for having read *Samson Agonistes*, but I am convinced that this is so.[5]

Finally, in his last critical essay, Eliot reiterates, in a more specific context of judgement, the earlier view he had expressed on Herbert:

> To understand Shakespeare we must acquaint ourselves
> with all of his plays; to understand Herbert we must
> acquaint ourselves with all of *The Temple*. Herbert is,
> of course, a much slighter poet than Shakespeare; never-
> theless he may justly be called a major poet.[6]

Eliot has described his criticism as a by-product of his poetic workshop. The self-deprecation in the phrase has tended to obscure the element of truth in it, which is that Eliot's criticism has always been enmeshed in a given literary situation and has found its strength because it has usually been charged with the forces needed to make that situation creative. Since part of the milieu which the criticism illuminates and moves forward is formed by Eliot's own poetry, it is reasonable that motifs predominant in the criticism should find their substantiation in the creative work. Those who regard 'Tradition and the Individual Talent' as the best of commentaries on *The Waste Land*, 'Dante' as the best commentary on *Ash-Wednesday*, and 'The Music of Poetry' as the best commentary on *Four Quartets* will not think it rash to sense in the passages quoted a clue to the understanding of Eliot's poetry as a whole. The implicit criterion is one of continuity, sometimes expressed in, but not necessarily identified with, the presence of a literary 'personality.' The important thing is that the continuity should possess the power of development, that it should be capable of creating and sustaining a significant process or a meaningful world.

Continuity is a concept which one tends to resist, partly because modern criticism has educated us so successfully in the self-sufficiency of the individual poem. It becomes desirable to tell ourselves that one critical hypothesis does not exclude the other and that because a work of art stands by itself it does not necessarily have to stand alone. Literature stripped of all contexts is unusual, if only because the language which enters literature is wrought from a context of both history and experience. Given the nearly unavoidable presence of a context, that of the œuvre can be as instructive and at least as fully designed as the context of genre or of milieu.

The problem for each poet is to find the right metaphor of wholeness, one that will grasp but not deform the poetry. One must also remember, though the warning may seem naïve, that poets write poems which are sometimes sheerly themselves and which decline to belong to anything larger. These eddies do not prove the absence of a mainstream; they merely add to it the richness of occasional dissent. Yet even the word 'mainstream' can be misleading, since the basic metaphor (or the figure, as Rosemond Tuve might call it) can be one of pattern as well as of movement or process. With Milton, for example, one thinks of five different literary forms reaching into a common centre of recognition; and the centre, if one may label it with the blatant crudeness demanded on these occasions, is that of man's responsibility for what he makes of himself. Each form conducts its exploration of this centre, according to its inheritance and resources. Each, so to speak, creates its own individual strategy of insight. The resultant literature is in a sense generic, but the collective design adds richness to the specific vistas opened by each form; and a powerful sense of inevitability is created as all roads end in the controlling truth. That this should happen is an aesthetic consequence of that massive and inclusive vision of order which Milton was perhaps the last man to feel in its entirety; wherever one begins and however one proceeds, one must in the end uncover the same pattern.[7]

With Yeats, more than one metaphor may be necessary, but one of the metaphors would be quasi-biological. The poetry is written out of a series of lived positions fitted into the trajectory of an individual life; and the whole truth is given by a series of lives fitted into the wheel of possibilities. Truth can only be experienced and not known; it cannot be talked about, but only presented and embodied. To live the truth is to live only part of it, because to live is to make choices, to accept exclusions, to be both the child and the victim of natural necessities. Man achieves his particular fragment and maximizes the size and validity of the fragment by moving through the possibilities that are permitted and by ensuring that each possibility is both completely and intensely lived.[8]

With Eliot, the curve of accomplishment is not based on the natural trajectory of life; its outline is rather that of an achieved and consolidated advance into knowledge. Each poem represents a step forward, or upward, building on the position won in the previous poem. The stairway is thus the vertebral metaphor, but the garden into which the stairway leads, the 'time of the tension between birth and dying,' is such that the perilous balance of understanding requires the quest to be entered again and its conclusions renewed. The movement of *Four Quartets* is more than merely cylic:

> We shall not cease from exploration
> And the end of all our exploring
> Will be to arrive where we started
> And know the place for the first time.

The shape of Eliot's poetry is thus composed by two forces: the spiral of process and the circle of design. Each necessitates the other and both stipulate the search for reality as a condition of man's being. It is not a search which can end in decisive findings: humankind cannot bear very much reality, and the enchainment of past and future protects mankind from heaven as well as from damnation. The sea of doubt is man's natural element, and the hints and guesses at the truth which illuminate that sea are designed not so much to end doubt as to save it from the whirlpool of despair. Eliot's poetry as an œuvre is thus given a unique and, as it were, double honesty, by its sense of a pattern won out of experience and by the manner in which the nature of the pattern entails a further commitment to experience through which the pattern is once again validated.

If these circumnavigations are not irrelevant, 'Prufrock' must take its place not simply as a beginning, but as a beginning which looks forward to an end, and which defines the terms of the unending inquiry. It has been remarked more than once that Prufrock's love song is never sung; what should be added is that his inability to sing it is not simply ironic, but part of the specifications of failure. To sing is to achieve a definition and Prufrock's fate is to fall short of definition, to bring momentous news only to thresholds. At the outset we are told that we will be taken through certain half-deserted streets

> that follow like a tedious argument
> Of insidious intent
> To lead you to an overwhelming question...

The slumming tour is also a return to underground life, and it is plain even at this stage that the overwhelming question is more than the proposal of marriage to a lady, that the love song must eventually be sung to Beatrice. In these circumstances Prufrock's 'Oh, do not ask, "What is it?"' is also more than a suggestion that the question will reveal itself as one strolls along. Much is in character here: the exaggeration that does not really exaggerate, the turning away from definition, and the implication that further inquiry would not be in good taste. We are in fact moving on two levels, and Prufrock's gestures, volubly in excess of the occasion, correlate fully to another order of reality which Prufrock unfortunately cannot confront and make explicit. He is too much the child of his milieu to achieve the outrageousness of proper definition, and since the ambience of 'Prufrock' is comic, the framing of the question must be an exercise in outrage, not as in *Gerontion*, a diagnosis of guilt. Eliot's favourite life-death ambiguity is potent here as nearly everywhere else. What seems to be life is death and to die into the true life one must die away from the salon. The paradox is sharpened at the climax of the poem when Prufrock drowns because he is awakened by human voices. But submarine or underground existence is not the answer and Prufrock does not undergo true death by drowning; the staircase he climbs is also, for the same reason, not a purgatorial stair. The reader is aware, through Prufrock, of the shocking nature of knowledge:

> Do I dare
> Disturb the universe?

But the scandal of recognition is beyond Prufrock himself. It is Lazarus and John the Baptist who are the proper ambassadors of reality to the salon, who can convey to it the angry, clawing truth. Prufrock still lives (and fails to live) by a minor and less taxing scale of values. Visions and decisions shade off into revisions. An eternal footman holds a coat, and the confession 'in short, I was afraid' reduces the deeper terror to everyday nervousness. 'Would it have been worth it, after all...?' Prufrock asks reassuringly, and the size of the exaggeration dismisses the enterprise:

To have squeezed the universe into a ball
To roll it towards some overwhelming question...

At a deeper level, however, the responsibility continues. The echo from Marvell reminds us that Marvell's suitor was more daring. As the poem develops, Prufrock's initial 'do not ask, "What is it?"' takes its proper place in the outline of failure. The overwhelming question has to be asked. It cannot be left to define or uncover itself. It must be forced into being in that passion for definition which seizes the moment and drives it to its crisis. The cost of definition will be more than ridicule. One is entitled to fear the cost. But not to meet it means the death of the man. The gesture of comic and yet of cosmic defiance – 'Do I dare/Disturb the universe?' – collapses now into mere sartorial rebellion:

Shall I part my hair behind? Do I dare to eat a peach?
I shall wear white flannel trousers, and walk upon the beach.

If the ambience of 'Prufrock' is comic, the Jacobean corridors of *Gerontion* are slippery with images of evasion and betrayal. Gerontion, an old man arithmetically, has known neither natural youth nor natural age. He is in fact that typical Eliot character who cannot die because he has not lived. The thought is mentioned in the second line and does not recur until the last line links the dry brain to the dry season. Cut off from the organic world, Gerontion is cut off also from the living truth, the sustaining sense of relatedness. He knows that Christ the tiger is also the helpless child of Lance-lot Andrewes's sermon;[9] but his mind cannot keep the paradox in balance, and as guilt drives him mercilessly against the wall it is the tiger that stalks through his unnatural year. The confrontation of reality cannot be endured; the images twist away into rites of expiation and anxiety, surrogates for the truth that will not be faced. It is this falling short, this failure of metaphysical nerve, that makes the difference between dying and dying into life. So the tree of life becomes the tree of wrath, and neither fear nor courage can save us, because both fear and courage acquire their full nature only when they are morally rooted.

The tiger springs in the new year. Us he devours.

This is the death of annihilation that looks forward to, yet is completely different from, another devouring in the desert by three white leopards. Gerontion's vehement declarations of design ('We have not reached conclusion. ... I have not made this show purposelessly'), with the repeated 'Think now' and the final 'Think at last' forcing the moment to its intellectual crisis, do seem to result in a last-minute facing of reality:

I would meet you upon this honestly.

But it is the honesty of the man against the wall, not that deeper confrontation which Eliot describes as 'that peculiar honesty, which, in a world too frightened to be honest, is peculiarly terrifying.' Gerontion's response is that of fear, not courage, in the metaphysical sense, and both its content and emptiness are pitilessly exposed in what is perhaps the most moving passage of the poem, as the imagery of old age blends into the sense of withering away from God:

I that was near your heart was removed therefrom
To lose beauty in terror, terror in inquisition.
I have lost my passion: why should I need to keep it

Since what is kept must be adulterated?
I have lost my sight, smell, hearing, taste and touch:
How should I use them for your closer contact?

In terms which are closer to the nerves of pity and terror, Gerontion's predicament is that of Prufrock.·He has moved forward in the act of definition, but he cannot cross the threshold, cannot make that surrender to reality which involves the death of the illusion which is his life. When the question is not asked the collapse into triviality must follow:

These with a thousand small deliberations
Protract the profit of their chilled delirium,
Excite the membrane, when the sense has cooled,
With pungent sauces, multiply variety
In a wilderness of mirrors.

Gerontion's frivolity may be more opulent than that of Prufrock, but the terms of failure are not dissimilar; the darker colouring is the result of a more sombre ambience, with the sense of guilt blocking the tentative effort at definition, just as the fear of ridicule did in the earlier poem. The death of the self follows the failure to achieve relationship, notwithstanding the multiplying of the self in mirrors; the poem's threatening rhetoric here calls for a grimmer extinction than Prufrock's elegant drowning. Gerontion's identity is disintegrated and even pulverized. His mind may have its fragments, but it is permitted no ruins against which to shore them, and the vestigial white feathers in the snow of oblivion, drawn into a gulf that is more than geographical, express vividly the sense of sheer obliteration, even down to the collapsing cadence.

When Pound dissuaded Eliot from making *Gerontion* a part of *The Waste Land*, he could not have been aware of the evolving logic of the œuvre.[10] Nevertheless, his action contributed to that logic. *Gerontion* looks forward to *The Waste Land* if only because there must be a world at the bottom of Dover cliff. Gerontion himself is unable to enter that world.

His monologue, made up of the thoughts 'of a dry brain in a dry season,' is carefully distanced from experience, and even the encounter to which he reaches imaginatively cannot be totally faced. To go forward from this point is to enter the abyss and to be prepared to prove nothingness on one's pulses. When one accepts the risk one also discovers that the risk is the only possibility of survival.

Seen in the symbolic continuum, the waste land is Prufrock's world more fully realized, a world where prophecy has fallen to fortune-telling, where love has hardened into the expertise of lust, where April is the cruellest month, and where the dead are no longer buried but planted in gardens. The fifth section is a break-out from this world, the dimensions of which are carefully controlled to fall short of a breakthrough. Because survival cannot be preached, but only endured, the mythologizing structure is crucially important in ensuring that whatever progress is achieved is not simply talked about, but lived through imaginatively. What the thunder says is the result of what the poem becomes, though, for reasons which will be apparent, the thunder speaks as a voice sought for by the poem but remaining outside it.

The Waste Land does not end where it begins. It may return to where it started with deeper understanding, but the mythodramatic progress is not depicted as circular. A journey to Chapel Perilous is undertaken, delirium and near-death evoke an ancient experience, a damp gust brings rain for which the limp leaves wait, the thunder speaks, proclaiming oracularly the conditions for deliverance, and the protagonist ends, fishing on the shore with the arid plain behind him. These are small gains but their very narrowness suggests their authenticity. As for the thunder, its pronouncements are designed to leave one in what Eliot once called a state of enlightened mystification.[11] Oracles achieve validity rather than clarity, and what they mean is decided by how experience reads them. One strong note in the voice of this oracle is a call to commitment – the awful daring of a moment's surrender, the recognition of the self as a prison, and the sea that would have been calm if one had chosen to venture on it, all seem to point straightforwardly in the same direction. When the protagonist decides to set his lands in order, as the bridges of the unreal city fall about him, we are witnessing the recovery of a traditional understanding. The collapse of civilization which a superficial reading (abetted by Eliot's notes) invites us to see here is also the death of an illusion, and reality can be born only from inward renewal.

The thunder speaks from the horizon of *The Waste Land* because what it has to say is discerned rather than experienced. The break-out from sterility is no more than that; it is not a movement into fruitfulness. The poem is an advance from *Gerontion*, building on that poem's terrified recognitions and taking the vital step forward from a condition in which neither fear nor courage can save us. Its conclusion sets the arid plain behind and moves us to the fringe of a world which the poem can formulate but cannot enter. To make that entrance is the function of *Ash-Wednesday*.

In *Ash-Wednesday* the protagonist endures a death unlike those suffered by Prufrock, Gerontion, and Phlebas and climbs a stair, decisively unlike that climbed by Prufrock, to the threshold of the overwhelming question. He reaches a garden, a precarious state of enlightenment, only to realize that the place of understanding must be held in constant struggle against the persistent downward pull of the flesh. He looks out finally on that sea of doubt and renewal where all that he has learned must be revalidated. It is repetition with a difference, the difference marking, with such precision as is possible, the movement forward in the life of the whole work. The death by devouring in *Ash-Wednesday* has a special place in this infra-structure. Unlike all previous dyings it is a dying into life; and its differences from Phlebas's death, which precedes it in the sequence, invite and respond to critical attention.

Phlebas too may owe his place in the œuvre to Pound, and Pound, whether he knew it nor not, was once again marking a turning point.[12] Phlebas's is the last of a series of old-style deaths, a warning of man's mortality, the inexorable reminder of the skull beneath the skin. Fear in a handful of dust is a step forward from the rather more animal fear of Gerontion, and the collocation of two mysticisms, as well as the play between purgatorial fire and the destructive fires of the flesh, points to the direction in which this fear can lead. It leads in fact to Chapel Perilous, but Phlebas's remains do not lie along this route. As a representative of that mercantile mentality for which the early poems preserve a special contempt, he is not permitted the consolation of any remains. De Bailhache, Fresca, and Mrs Cammel are despatched into outer space and disintegrated into 'fractured atoms' in what seems a reasonably thorough process of destruction. But Phlebas has his bones picked for fourteen days by the mocking whispers of a current under sea and then enters a whirlpool, where he is presumably churned into a further refinement of non-being. In *Ash-Wednesday* the death rites may be superficially as gruesome, but the total effect is of a curious, limpid happiness. Despite its relevance, one would hesitate to use the word 'gaiety' if the voice of the thunder had not legitimized it. It is, in fact, something akin to Yeats's 'gaiety transfiguring all that dread' that lies on the other side of radical commitment, though to reach that other side one must pass through an experience, translatable only by the metaphor of death. The verse, by the manner in which its singing sweetness lives through and overrides the macabre narrative, embodies fully the elusive sense of metamorphosis into a higher reality. In what is later to be described as 'A condition of complete simplicity/Costing not less than everything' there is a kind of lucid, tranquil givenness, symbolized in the creative destitution of the landscape. To be aware of this it is not necessary to assign specific functions to the leopards; the number three is sufficiently evocative. As for the indigestible portions which the leopards reject, these may represent a residue of the self which survives destruction, but they also surely stand for the difference between mere dying and dying into life. Two significant links in the chain remain to be added. First, the prison of the self is broken – the bones are united by their forgetfulness of themselves and each other. Second, the protagonist's cry in *The Waste Land* – 'Shall I at least set my lands in order?' – is answered by: 'This is the land. We have our inheritance.' As understanding passes into experience the ruined tower becomes the tradition redeemed.

Man's mind was not born for peace. It inhabits a time of tension and a place of twilight. To die into life, it renounces everything, including renunciation. Then, reborn, it must climb a stairway, along which the process of struggle and rejection is once again enacted. The higher reality may be given to us eventually, but it is not given for settlement. The desert is in the garden and the garden in the desert. The withered appleseed of our failing may be spat out but there is every possibility that the seed will flourish again. In the story of the quest, the chapter called *Ash-Wednesday* has a certain stubborn honesty because of its quiet demonstration that the only end to the quest is its renewal.

The very title of *Four Quartets* implies repetition, and the epigraph from Heraclitus, the Yin and Yang of the inverted mottoes that enclose *East Coker*, the images of circular and spiral movement, the persistent metaphors of journeying, not only take up and consummate a literary past already familiar and achieved, but also make real the involvement of pattern in process. 'In my beginning is my end' speaks from the biological as well as the unchanging world. The detail of the pattern is movement, and even that love which is beyond all movement is caught in limitation between unbeing and being. The moment of enlightenment is in and out of time, half heard in the stillness between two waves of the sea.

Since it is only through time that time is conquered, there can be no alternative or end to exploration. We begin in a house with a settled order and a formal garden, with meditations precise and tentative. Innocence inhabits the garden and enlightenment may return to it; but to live in a house is to learn that one must leave it, to make the discovery that 'houses live and die.' The sense of design must reassert itself in a circle of experience, slowly widening and increasingly corrosive. The houses of *East Coker* face the sea, and the protagonist, middle-aged like Prufrock, looks out over the vast waters, hearing not the fluting voices of mermaids, but the 'wave cry' and the 'wind cry,' through the empty desolation. Whatever understanding one achieves has been lived through and must therefore be left behind; the future is always a new beginning and a different failure. *The Dry Salvages* accepts the inevitable journey, committing the protagonist to that perilous ocean on which the houses of *East Coker* and the rocks of *Ash-Wednesday* look. Both the river within us and the sea around us are made to live as forces of chaos, attacking and eroding the boundaries of order. As the second section of the poem tolls in the accumulated rhythm of the meaningless, we are brought again to the landscape of destitution, the world of bleached bones and sand, and the overwhelming question, where the sense of form becomes the will to survive.

At the margin, small movements are decisively significant. They mark the difference between life and death, between despair and indestructible meaning. On this beach, as in the desert of *Ash-Wednesday*, the poetry centres its weight of realization and its power to resist defeat on minute gains, defined with the precision of the authentic. The 'unprayable/ Prayer' becomes the 'hardly, barely prayable/Prayer.' The 'calamitous annunciation' becomes the 'one annunciation.' The protagonist who in *East Coker* felt the world become 'stranger' and the pattern 'more complicated' is now reassured because a pattern exists which is not a mere sequence or a development. There is a meaning not given *by* but given *to* experience, as is clear from this particular section of *The Dry Salvages*.

At the edge of nothingness, the birth of meaning (or the refusal of the indigestible portions to die) takes place in a manner both creative and ancient. Poetry cannot report the event; it must *be* the event, lived through in a form that can speak about itself while remaining wholly itself. This is a feat at least as difficult as it sounds, and if the poem succeeds in it, it is because, however much it remembers previous deaths by drowning, it creates its own life against its own thrust of questioning. The careful separation of enlightenment from any possible 'meaning' of happiness is typical of the specificity achieved.[13] At the same time the reader is conscious of a momentum which gained force before the poem and will endure beyond it. What is said here acquires additional power, because the literary past, the life of the œuvre, has a pattern that is not a mere sequence and cannot be called development.

The Dry Salvages represents the maximum horizon of *Four Quartets*. When the sea of nihilism (only Arnold saw it as a sea of faith) has been denied its total victory, elemental time, older than the time of chronometers, civilizes itself into historic time, and past, present, and future are found again in an organic relationship. This is one man's way of knowing that

> If you came this way,
> Taking any route, starting from anywhere,
> At any time, or at any season
> It would always be the same...

The circle completes itself or, to put it differently, contracts to the point which is its centre. We end as we begin, entering the unknown, remembered gate to the garden. But we also end, knowing the unity between the fire of energy and the rose of perfect form.

A critical metaphor sufficient to compass Eliot's poetry has its betrayals as well as its excitements. If it is not kept in its place, it may impose upon the work an obsessive logic and an intolerable tidiness. To lay down such Procrustean definitions is no part of the business of this chapter. All that is suggested is that such metaphors are possible and that they have their role in shaping critical perceptions. The interpretations of *Gerontion* and 'Prufrock' offered here, for example, differ from customary readings; but they fit the facts as well as any alternatives and enable the facts themselves to be fitted into a larger pattern. *The Waste Land* and *Ash-Wednesday* also gain in richness and in solidity when we are aware of the total life from which they issue and against which they are set. Whether such increments are aesthetic in nature (or indeed whether they are increments at all) is, of course, for the reader to judge. At any rate this book pays Eliot the courtesy of taking him at his word on the difference between major and minor achievement.

In a tentative exploration, not every fact can be decisively located, and some facts, as has already been suggested, are part of the poet's right to forget his own patterns, whether known or instinctive. Certain other poems will not be considered, not because they are in conflict with the metaphor studied here, but because they do not contribute to it as characteristically as the poems chosen. The plays are a different problem and perhaps require a metaphor of their own. This is not to suggest that Eliot's dramatic and poetic concerns are dissimilar; the point is that the force of continuity in the drama calls for a different specification. What should have emerged with some firmness from this chapter is Eliot's remarkable power of wholeness. His work is not simply a series of individual excellences but a totality fully experienced and almost painfully lived through. The movement suggested here, the carefully built trajectory of understanding, the attainment of enlightenment under conditions that compel the quest to be re-enacted, the circle closed and yet forever open, all point to a design too subtle and too organic to be planned. What we are facing is what, in another context, has been interestingly called the artifice of reality.

Eliot's essay on Pascal has an unmistakable eloquence of involvement. Reading it, we are always aware that what he says applies to more than his subject. Nowhere is this clearer than in the following remarks:

> every man who thinks and lives by thought must have his own scepticism, that which stops at the question, that which ends in denial, or that which leads to faith and which is somehow integrated into the faith which transcends it. And Pascal, as the type of one kind of religious believer, which is highly passionate and ardent, but passionate only through a powerful and regulated intellect, is in the first sections of his unfinished Apology for Christianity facing unflinchingly the demon of doubt which is inseparable from the spirit of belief.[13]

The parallels are evident and revealing. Eliot's poetry is a process of living by thought, of seeking to find peace 'through a satisfaction of the whole being.' It is singular in its realization of passion through intelligence. It is driven by a scepticism which resolutely asks the question but refuses to stop short at it, by a sensibility sharply aware of 'the disorder, the futility, the meaninglessness, the mystery of life and suffering.' If it attains a world of belief or a conviction of order, that conviction is won against the attacking strength of doubt and remains always subject to its corrosive power. Not all of us can share Eliot's faith. But all of us can accept the poetry because nearly every line of it was written while looking into the eyes of the demon.

CHAPTER TWO

The Dialect of the Tribe

Twenty years after the writing of *The Waste Land* a man treads the street of an unreal city where the dead leaves rattle like tin over the asphalt. Death has undone many who flowed over London Bridge and much more than the bridge is tumbling down. The rain for which the limp leaves of the jungle had waited is now the fiery rain that falls on a burning metropolis. The thunder that spoke will be the dove descending. Midwinter Spring has superseded April as the season of cruelty and creativeness. At the heart of light, the hyacinth has become the lotus and the rose.

These detailed relationships make it evident that we have reached a turning of the stair and are invited to look down on what has been passed through. But in looking down we do not merely see a province of the mind more clearly because we see it in a light that is closer to finality. We are also made to recognize that the winding stair has been travelled by others, who contemplate what we understand through our own eyes and help us to draw the shape of an understanding which is both within us and beyond ourselves. The familiar compound ghost is a reminder of how the historical sense calls on us to respond to the presence of the past as well as to its pastness. Unidentifiable because it is intimate, it is so much a part of the writer's being that to discourse with it is virtually to assume a double part in the dialogue with one's self.

It is possible to apply some useless scholarship to the delineating of those 'brown, baked features' but there are certain basic resemblances which it is instructive as well as intriguing to discern. To talk about the bitterness of age and the wreckage of the body is to summon to the stair the poetry of Yeats, but more is involved than this unavoidable acknowledgement. The style of the encounter itself evokes the elder poet's views upon the mask, while differentiating Eliot's treatment from that of Yeats. The reference to 'the rending pain of re-enactment' recalls with exactness the anguish of *Purgatory*. The mention of 'honour' reminds us of the *Dialogue of Self and Soul*, with honour finding the self in the wintry blast. The exasperated spirit proceeding from wrong to wrong directs us once again to *Purgatory* and to the climax which extends the chain of error in seeking to cut it. The dancer is one of Yeats's more celebrated images, and the dancer in the fires of purification is the summit of the upward effort in *Byzantium*. Others besides Yeats have blown their horns in poetry but, given the accumulations of detail, it may not be without significance that the 'fabulous horn' in Yeats is linked to the 'sudden shower.'[1]

There is, however, another remembrance in the compound ghost that haunts Eliot more tellingly and creatively than Yeats. Though Laforgue taught Eliot 'how to speak' and Baudelaire showed him 'the possibility of fusion between the sordidly realistic and the phantasmagoric'[2] which he put to such decisive use in *The Waste Land*, it was Dante who, after forty years, remained 'the most persistent and deepest influence' on his work. It was, moreover, a cumulative influence: 'the older you grow, the stronger the domination becomes.'[3] The encounter scene in *Little Gidding* – the closest approximation that has been achieved in English to the effect of *terza rima* in Italian – pays appropriate tribute to this influence. Twenty years ago it was Dante's words which were chosen to characterize the unreal city and to suggest in the last lines of the poem the means of escape from that city into reality. *Little Gidding* confirms the conjecture that it is Dante, rather than Stetson, who has been with the poet in the ships at Mylae. But the dead master's presence is not easy to accommodate, and Eliot admits that this section of *Little Gidding* 'cost me far more time and trouble and vexation than any passage of the same length that I had ever written.'[4] We can either pine for the discarded drafts or respond to the tautness and the fluency which is the result of all this stitching and unstitching. Whatever our preferences, we would be less than just if we did not discern that the thing said is as Dantesque as the way of saying it, particularly in the final recurrence of those lines from the twenty-sixth canto of the *Purgatorio* which have so dominated Eliot's creative memory.

This crucial passage provides the title for the third volume of poems that Eliot published in England. A line from it appears in one of the discarded poems in the *Waste Land* manuscript. A phrase furnishes yet another title, this time for a section of *Ash-Wednesday* as it was first published. A further phrase is embodied in the text of another section. Finally, the crucial line in which the ghost tells us that deliverance from error is only possible when we make ourselves new in the refining fire is one of those carefully chosen fragments which the protagonist in *The Waste Land* shores against his ruins.[5] The advance into meaning so scrupulously achieved by the intervening poetry invites us again to look down the stairway and to understand more fully what the thunder said.

The third ingredient in the ghost is not altogether expected. Laforgue may have taught Eliot how to speak but it is Mallarmé, not Laforgue, who tells us what it means to be concerned with speech. We know that Eliot came to prefer Mallarmé to Laforgue as he came to prefer Herbert to Donne.[6] But the ghost is not compounded as it is, merely to state Eliot's preferences. It stands in the poem to declare the poem's nature and the nature of those previous acts of exploration that have helped to make possible whatever truth is found here. A varied company is joined and justly joined in the unearthly community where two worlds overlap. We find the arch-symbolist and the poet who moved beyond symbolism in order to find that he had no speech but symbol. There is the poet of the rose and the poet who cultivated the rose, in learning how the holy tree grows like the lotus in man's heart. There are two men who cast their lives into their rhymes and whose rhymes tell of more than medieval Florence and the indomitable Irishry. There are the swordsman, the saint and the aesthete, the poet of the swan and of the swan in shadow. In responding to a collective presence which the poem rightly describes as 'both one and many,' we learn something of the width of a poet's apprenticeship and of the responsibility laid on us in our concern with speech.

Concern with speech is also made evident by the manner in which three of the *Four Quartets* turn to the discussion of language during their final sections, moving first through its betrayals and then to its fulfilment in the complete consort dancing together, the commerce of high and low as well as of old and new. The formal decorum points as it must to the deeper coherence to which it is connected. Since its symbol is the dance, we are called on to remember that the dance in the same three Quartets has been used to signify matrimony, the meeting of stillness and motion, and the joining of two worlds in measured movement through the purgatorial fire. Thus, even the tactics of speech enact the recognitions which speech seeks to convey. Our concern is with words because for those born to use them, words are the best way of finding what stands at the centre of the wheeling and turning of words.

The ghost's next line raises a variety of interesting issues entangled in a manner which we must hopefully call creative. Since Eliot associated himself with a revolution in poetry characterized by a return to the language of common speech,[7] we might argue that his main aim in poetry was to restore rather than to purify dialect. But poetic language in its remoter reaches – and it is also the language of a tribe in this sense – has itself been castigated as a Babylonish dialect harsh and barbarous.[8] Are we then concerned with a golden mean or 'an easy commerce,' anticipated by previous efforts to raise the vernacular into literary dignity? This is the accomplishment frequently credited to Dante in Italian and Ben Jonson in English. We can observe with scholarly prudence that this is undoubtedly part of what the ghost meant, particularly if we supplement our caution with the platitude that the boundaries of the vernacular are indefinite. Though large slabs of dialect were eliminated in the final version of *The Waste Land*,[9] enough remains to instruct us on the function of low life in high poetry. Yet *The Waste Land* is not simply a twentieth-century achievement in the plain style, and though Eliot can affirm that 'history is now and England' we refrain from underlining too heavily the Englishness of Eliot. Perhaps we restrain ourselves because the ghost has convinced us.

The word 'tribe' is generously inclusive in the first place. Dante, Mallarmé, and Yeats have different ways of purifying dialect. But if we extend the term even further to cover the efforts of all those who think and live by thought, the followers of the lotus and the rose, of Buddha, of Krishna, and of Augustine, if we think of the many dialects of comprehension behind which stands the unchanging language of truth, we see more and see better in looking down the stairway. The fragment from Heraclitus which forms the first of the epigraphs to *Four Quartets* supports such a reading. So too does the ghost's suggestion that the purpose of purifying the tribe's dialect is 'to urge the mind to aftersight and foresight.'

Eliot's poetry is an advance, an inch-by-inch movement up the stairway in which the end is significant because it both remembers and fulfils the beginning. 'The end is where we start from' and therefore to some degree the final cause which defines the full accomplishment. Though *The Waste Land* largely stands by itself, it is not fully itself until it is placed in a continuum and until we look back on it along what the later work discloses as the path of its potentiality, the direction it must take to achieve its own becoming.

Enough has been said to allow the simplification that the poet advances from dialect into speech and eloquence, and more particularly into that deeper eloquence which is the discovery and celebration of the meaningful. One way of considering *The Waste Land* is to see it as assiduously assembling the potential components of that eloquence. We encounter in it the polyglot poem ranging laterally across cultures, ranging backwards into the literary past and ranging up and down the social ladder through the disguises and declarations of emptiness. The effort at inclusiveness is strenuous. Significance should come out of the talk and the gestures, out of the relics of meaning which the mind has sifted through and the memory hoarded. The directing voice is civilized enough and has travelled sufficiently far to be dissatisfied with Burbank and his Baedeker. All it lacks are the resources of speech, the shared understanding between man and man, or even the pattern given to the mind within which the mind's contents can be located and understood. The units of awareness may be present but what cannot quite be achieved are the connective forces, the grammar of comprehension.

This is modern man and the sound of the key turning is the proof of a prison which might otherwise not be recognized. This is man not only east of Eden, but probably too far east of it for creative or even for nostalgic remembrance. Paradise is not lost but destroyed, as it is at a decisive moment in Milton's poem. The mind can voyage through the strange seas of itself. It will find not Ithaca, but a whirlpool.

Ithaca in our time has been a popular destination. The shaping presence of the *Odyssey* is of course prominent in Joyce and Pound, and Eliot's claim that we must use the mythical instead of the narrative method is frequently intoned, though some doubt can be expressed about the degree of method in his myths. What is also important is the strong recollection, in the discarded drafts of *The Waste Land*, of Ulysses's final voyage as recounted by Dante. The Dry Salvages are a milestone in that voyage,[10] so it is no accident that the third Quartet sets before us a journey to the limits of the known and a death by drowning which, unlike the death of Phlebas the Phoenician, is what Marvell would call a shipwreck into health. There are other recollections which are also evolutions. Belladonna, the lady of the rocks, becomes the lady whose shrine stands on the promontory. The *Gita* supersedes the Fire Sermon. The three imperatives which end *The Waste Land* – give, sympathize, control – are replaced by 'Ardour and selflessness and self-surrender.' Finally, Madame Sosostris (or rather her paraphernalia) make what can only be called an appropriate reappearance at a time when Hitler was busy with his astrologers. But the inventory of clairvoyant tactics – Eliot's parody of the epic catalogue – takes place *after* that death by water which Madame Sosostris had warned us to avoid. We are therefore no longer prisoners of the parody but are able to see beyond it and to reach around it to the truth which it deforms but also hints at. We learn the limitations of that dimension which man's curiosity searches but to which it also clings. There is more than one way in which the coming of Christ can silence the oracles.

We have moved forward from *The Waste Land* in taking up some of its images, and how we have moved forward is suggested by a crucial passage in *The Dry Salvages*:

> We had the experience but missed the meaning,
> And approach to the meaning restores the experience
> In a different form, beyond any meaning
> We can assign to happiness. I have said before
> That the past experience revived in the meaning
> Is not the experience of one life only
> But of many generations...

We may note in passing how 'many generations' reminds us of the multiple ingredients of the familiar compound ghost, of the citations of the past that in *The Waste Land* flow into and frame the sterile present, and of that simultaneous presence of the totality of literature which constitutes tradition for the individual talent. But our immediate concern must be those insistent intertwinings which bind experience and meaning together in spreading yet gathered relationships, so that we are made aware of meaning as something both attained by experience and itself experienced. We recall that thought, to Donne, was an experience which modified his sensibility. Thus the pattern by which language is able to touch the central stillness cannot be imposed. We also stand at a point in the mind's history where the pattern can no longer be assumed or even discovered. The main intermediate possibility is the one taken up by Eliot's poetic development. If meaning cannot be found it must be heard. The search for significance must be driven forward to a boundary at which the thunder can legitimately speak.

It is in the end not simply Madame Sosostris, but the poetic act in its stubborn integrity, which clings to the dimension of past and future. That clinging is not necessarily a failing. It must be seen against a complementary truth which Eliot's writing also puts to us, which is that time is only conquered through time. If the birth of meaning is to take place at the edge of experience, then experience itself must find its way to the edge. The poem of the whole mind, which *The Waste Land* certainly is in a crucial sense, must end in the partial defeat of the mind. But the defeat would be frustrating rather than creative if the poem did not proceed to it and to some degree achieve it through a full and honest exposure of the mind's contents.

It is necessary to put everything on the table and in this sense the polyglot poem is today's version of the encyclopedic epic. It too, like *Paradise Lost*, attempts to be the infinite receptacle, but its principles of organization are not evident from its credentials. The traditional poem either declares itself or puts forward and progressively puts together the ingredients of an understanding that is able to complete and to shape it. *The Waste Land* is purposefully limited to ascertaining the conditions under which understanding might be reached. To proceed even this far and to know itself even to this degree, it must call upon everything in the mind that seems capable of significance and, having convened itself, subject itself to scrutiny. It is east of Babel as well as east of Eden. If the possibility of speech exists, it can only exist at the heart of the medley of voices.

It is not only the landscape of *The Waste Land* to which we should attend. The earth thirsting for rain is the mind thirsting for meaning. To find a structure not alien to itself it must put down the nuclei of significance, the broken images in their felt juxtapositions, shuffling them like cards and rearranging them like tea leaves. It must widen its resources, the hinterland by which it is civilized. Many languages and the literature of many periods can uncover between themselves more surely the principles by which the mind is made. Wisdom should be the accumulation of many dialects, the gist of the best that has been known and thought. Or is it, ironically, lodged in the mind's trivia? The search for significance would be less than conclusive if it did not take in all pertinent possibilities.

It is apparent by now that the search has to fail. To say this is not to imply that it was designed to fail, or even that what the failure meant was seen with clarity at the time of the failure. A boundary is reached, and it is only by looking backwards from what is subsequently achieved beyond the boundary that we understand the poem which the boundary encloses. When we have been led to aftersight we are able to recognize that the failure must be comprehensive in order to be meaningful. Until the possibilities of the dimension are exhausted, the mind's curiosity will cling to past and future. More than one journey is needed before it can reach the conclusion that it cannot know its nature through its geography.

Despite appearances, the poetry of failure is by no means easy to write. The finding of meaning is so bound up with the achievement of form that it can seem to be part of a poem's natural destiny. Doubt may threaten the poem but the climactic chords resound. Moreover, at the time that Eliot wrote *The Waste Land*, an accomplished failure-artist, W.B. Yeats, was turning failure into his greatest success. At the other extreme the failure of incompetence is easy enough to avoid; but the failure of meaninglessness, of an abyss so deep that the thunder cannot speak to it, must also be turned aside though the poem may be called on by its integrity to confront it. The ironies of a poem such as *The Waste Land* can be made to circumvent this threat by implying more than the participating voices are capable of saying. But these ironies must carefully stop short of defining shaping principles, limiting themselves to the recognitions which will enable those principles to be announced and to be placed in relation to the poem's necessities.

Even the 'placing' may be something which other poems in the continuum have to accomplish. What the thunder says is a succession of imperatives, not necessarily felt as more authentic than the poem's other voices. The response is the familiar disjointedness, the shoring of fragments in a gesture like those many other gestures to which the poem has fruitlessly submitted. If more is meant, it is the turn in the stairway which shows us what else has entered our condition.

To this extent criticisms of *The Waste Land* that draw attention to its residual unrelatedness, to the failure of its various elements to cohere, testify obliquely to the poem's integrity. It can indeed be argued without perversity that *The Waste Land* not only has to fail but fail in the particular way in which it does fail if it is to prepare the way for the movement forward in subsequent poems and so take its proper and productive place within the achievement of the poetry as a whole. What is important is that the elements in *The Waste Land* should be brought together not so as to achieve a meaning, but to particularize an experience and a dialect which will make possible an advance into meaning and speech. The poem is not self-sufficient. It is part of a progress which began before it and will continue beyond it. Gerontion's phrase 'We have not reached conclusion' – a phrase which his own withering away from the source of life has emptied – is one which it is the concern of the whole movement to restore.

It is for this reason that, despite Eliot's brave words in his *Dial* review of *Ulysses*, the mythical method can be no more successful than the narrative method. It does not control, order, and give significance to the immense panorama of futility and anarchy which is contemporary history.[11] It is, in fact, an arrangement rather than a structure. Similarly deceptive is the observation in the footnotes on the locus of *The Waste Land*. What Tiresias sees may very well be the whole poem, but what he sees is not meaningful unless it is found in the poem. That it is not found suggests that the integrative force of vision is alien to the poem on its chosen plane of existence; it is an alienation embodied in the emptiness of the poem's ritual gestures of renewal. These gestures were once life-giving acts. But in the climate of the waste land, divination has been debased into fortune-telling and love has been mechanized as lust. The connections with the past fail to provide a basis for transformation. They define the diminuendo of the present but the music they invoke is louder rather than different: the bang is not superior to the whimper. Fear in a handful of dust may seem to promise something in its menaces, but it is actually closer to Gerontion's sterile terror than it is to the creative fear of the holy. The cage in which the Sibyl wished to die serves not to intensify the longing for escape but to provide instead, according to the manuscript, the setting for the calculations of a chess game.[12] Even that celebrated collocation of 'two representatives of eastern and western asceticism,' which Eliot heavily advises us is not accidental, does not provide us with the terms of renewal. It is the sense of destruction which is dominant in the immediacies of the verse, with the word 'burning' standing finally in isolation as if all qualifications to it had been burned away. The restorative implications which the thought can carry (as in Donne's fourteenth sonnet or in *Good Friday Riding Westward*) remain indecisive in the verbal energies. If we remind ourselves of the relationship between burning and refining, we must also recognize that the poem's progress so far has not achieved possession of that relationship. Thus when death comes in the next section, its implications are limited to a studious reminder of the skull beneath the skin. There are no dolphins to carry Phlebas to Byzantium and no voice to assure us that Lycidas is not dead. The great vision of the guarded mount may stand at the horizon of the poem in what the thunder says, but only when the poem has exhausted its own insufficiency.

It remains to us to consider the words heard in the voice of the thunder and the sequence in which they are heard. Eliot's reference to the *Brihadaranyaka Upanishad* is inaccurate,[13] so it can be argued that in altering the order of the three imperatives he was merely providing us with a second case of faulty recollection. The Editorial Board which produced *The Waste Land* was not infallible, and one of the words in the fragment from the *Pervigilium Veneris* is persistently misquoted in the manuscripts.[14] The Board has no comment on what the thunder said unless Pound's 'O.K. from here on *I think*'[15] is taken as applying to the whole final section. But perhaps the altered order can be made to submit to a better explanation than individual forgetfulness and collective negligence.

The thunder's single seed-word, DA, is apprehended in three ways by three orders of existence. The Gods hear it as *Damyata*, man as *Datta*, and the Asuras as *Dayadhvam*. This is the sequence in the Sanskrit, and it has the obvious advantage of providing us with an orderly descent through the scale of existence as well as with an indication of the main shortcoming of each of the three orders. Eliot begins with man. and it can be argued that he does so not because of reckless egocentricity but because all three imperatives are heard in the poem as addressed to the human condition.

A further and more important justification of the sequence is that it enables Eliot to put 'control' (*Damyata*) at the end, and it is precisely control which the poem has failed to achieve in contemplating and ransacking its contents and in administering to them the vestigial rites of renewal. Moreover, two movements of commitment now precede the attainment of control, and it can be suggested that the former bring about the latter. The elaboration of *Datta* is heavily revised in the manuscript and it is apparent that changes such as 'blood shaking the heart' for 'blood beating in the heart' and 'can never retract' for 'cannot retract' are made to increase the intensity of commitment. In the comment on *Dayadhvam*, the deletion of 'friend, my friend' stresses the isolation of the prison of the self; the same effect is underlined by the replacement of 'murmurs' by 'rumours'; and the substitution of 'confirms a prison' for 'has built a prison' indicates that the first stage in the liberation of ourselves must come from the recognition of our own imprisonment.[16] All the restorative efforts in the waste land have in truth been acts of self-immurement, fearing the flow of life, coveting the dead gestures, degrading love into lust, contemplating only as annihilation what could be the passage to a fuller and higher existence, till we reach a point where the voice of the thunder is needed to remind us that we once heard the sound of the key turning. Only by blood shaking the heart, by an act of reaching out deep enough to imperil the structures of our lives, can we re-establish the conditions of our being.

As the re-establishment takes place, the commitment beyond the self and the abandonment of the self result not in the losing but in the finding of control. The sea is calm enough for gaiety to transfigure what on the other side of the venture seemed like dread.[17] The 'you' of the third declension (contrasted with the 'we' of the first and the 'I' of the second) enables us to imagine that the thunder is addressing the speaker of the last lines. The speaker would then be one who had been unable to make the transforming commitment. This is not the effect of the earlier stages of the manuscript, but the revisions may well have been directed to securing such an effect.[18]

The final words are a promise of control, preceded by acts which seem to establish its opposite and succeeded by images in which the old disintegration appears to return and even to be intensified. As the end loops back to the beginning, we are invited to ask ourselves whether we only see a deeper chaos or whether we are able to know the place for the first time. The appearances are those of fragmentation, a delirious babble effective only in suggesting that Hieronimo has attained the peace of madness. If the thunder had not spoken it would be no more than ingenious to point out that the arid plain is now behind the speaker, or that the erstwhile heap of broken images is now *shored* against his ruins in what may be read as an initial act of retrieval. Since the thunder has spoken we are able to see how, at the poem's limit, the promise of control announces itself notwithstanding and even paradoxically because of the images of fragmentation with which it is juxtaposed. We realize that 'Shall I at least set my lands in order' is more than an inquiry as to what can be saved from the holocaust. Behind the ingrained habits of the waste land, the clutching at personal identity and private relics, there remains the possibility of inner restoration. A later poem will say 'This is the land. We have our inheritance,'[19] and the modulation will define how experience misses the meaning.

If we consider the shored fragments as the lands which are set in order – a construction which intensifies the movement of disintegration with which the poem ends on one of its levels – we can see how the fire which Arnaut Daniel enters extends the teachings of 'The Fire Sermon' and will, in its turn, extend into the many meanings of fire which dance in *Little Gidding* round the revival of the same words. To be young like the swallow, the aged eagle must refuse to stretch its wings. He who was advised to guard against death by water must learn in *Ash-Wednesday* to accept death by devouring and must learn in *The Dry Salvages* how to submit and what is achieved by submission to the onslaught of that sea which is all about us. The ruined tower, already the symbolic home of another poet, will be found in *Ash-Wednesday* to conceal a winding stair. Though it leads into a garden, a further cycle of poems will make it clear that the peace of the garden can only be momentary, and that we must embark upon a perilous flood, more threatening and therefore more life-giving than the waste land's sterility. If traditions have been found wanting, it is so that a dead master can instruct a living pupil in what is truly creative in the presence of the past. To study the shored fragments is to appreciate that to make an end (in both senses) is truly to make a beginning; but the realization is brought about by the pointing forward of the poem even more than by its self-evaluative ironies.

The dimension must be searched and its failings felt. Its rites of renewal must be tested and found insufficient. At the edge to which the poem brings itself another dimension can then be manifested, declaring at the point of intersection what is latent in the experience that seems to have been explored. It is typical of the integrity of the poem we are considering that even at this point the meaning is not triumphantly proclaimed. It is not even indisputably recognized. When the declensions of the thunder are repeated in the last lines, it is almost as if they were another series of fragments, part of the lands which are to be set in order instead of the shaping principles which are to order those lands. The final benediction – 'Shantih, Shantih, Shantih' – can be read as reflecting the peace of enlightenment, or as indicating no more than exhausted subsidence into a consolatory formula, a termination rather than an ending. We are left with the débris of dialect. If the terms of renewal have been heard on the poem's horizon, it is the subsequent poems that Eliot writes which, by embodying the advance into meaning and speech, will enable us to look back on an earlier journey and to see its significance 'in a different form.'

In recent years there has been a growing understanding that Eliot's works compose a continuity and that his individual poems can only be fully themselves when they are placed and explored in that continuity. 'The constituent things,' F.R. Leavis writes, 'are in their concentration so completely what they are, the development is so unforeseeable, and yet so compelling in its logic, that the whole body of the poetry affects us as one astonishing major work.'[20] Frank Kermode comments that 'when the Quartets speak of a pattern of timeless moments, of the point of intersection, they speak *about* the pattern and that point; the true image of them is *The Waste Land*. There the dreams cross. the dreams in which begin responsibilities.'[21] The previous chapter of this book, first published in 1966, has sought to characterize the concerns that underlie and integrate Eliot's poetry. A fuller examination of *The Waste Land* helps to define an important stage in the response of a mind, distinctive both in its tenacity and in its literary percipience, to the overwhelming questions by which its growth was shaped.

CHAPTER THREE

The Twilight Kingdom

A poet of major accomplishment advances initially through the minor genres sometimes professing to write with forced fingers and lamenting his inadequacy for the exercise he triumphantly performs. At length he equips himself for the poem of highest hope and hardest attempting not simply because he is technically proficient, but because the assault of life has been endured and the frames of order still remain in being. Eliot's work does not move through a sequence of resounding affirmations but it meets the terms of progress in a world of which the Hollow Men are to whisper the terminal cadences. Through the comic failure of Prufrock, the tragic failure of Gerontion, and the epic-encyclopedic failure of *The Waste Land* an advance is made to a threshold at which the thunder can speak, not to declare the shape of things, but to suggest the rites of passage which are necessary in order to know any shape. Consistent with this 'progress' through what are appropriately gestures rather than genres is a movement through a fitting sequence of agents – Prufrock in middle age, Gerontion in old age, and finally Tiresias who is beyond age, the proper observer of the eternal recurrence. The pattern of time is not to be discerned by those who in the nature of experience are time's prisoners. It is to be discerned only through a creative relationship with a force beyond time by which time is penetrated.

The movement thus achieved is a fastidiously wrought, carefully measured advance in which experience is given its opportunity to achieve a meaning other than futility. And since Eliot learnt from his Elizabethan mentors, the advance is not restricted to a single line of movement. Apeneck Sweeney guards the gates of horn while Prufrock performs between the gates of ivory. Rachel née Rabinovitch, tearing at the grapes with murderous paws, has the prehensile energy Prufrock dreamed of in those ragged claws scuttling across the floors of silent seas. Sweeney's world thus complements the world of the sophisticates, putting it to us that understanding is not to be found by descending lower. The quatrains in which Sweeney is observed (and which Eliot took from Gautier)[1] expound a bleak geometry complementing the futilities of Prufrock's salon, a bleakness which the participants as well as the observer come to see. Given these relationships, it seems only fitting that muscle should perform in these stanzas of athletic animality while the mind plays out its superior diversions in *vers libre*. Two different styles concur in the same discovery. The pulsation of things must be felt in its inescapability and Sweeney's cannibal isle may be the place in which to feel it, particularly when one is relieved of the distractions of the world's best books. Parallels duly insinuate themselves. There is cannibalism also in Prufrock's visions and revisions. Nightingales sing in both worlds, ignored in one, derided in the other, telling of expiation and of transformation. A knock at the door can relieve the boredom, or usher in the terror. Birth and copulation and death is a condition from which the Fire Sermon preaches deliverance. That the mind should divest itself of the love of created things, as the epigraph to *Sweeney Agonistes* tells us, is a lesson not learnt by Gerontion, that obsessive conservationist.

When parallel movements advance into congruent understandings the force of the conclusions those understandings lead to is strengthened. But the critic examining these paral-

lels is not simply laying bare a series of prudent reinforce-
ments. A world must be adequately populated and the dra-
matised evidence in it must be reasonably representative if we
are to accept as valid the sense of its incarceration in its own
mindless cycles. We must be brought to see and not simply
through the juxtapositions of the Fire Sermon, the imprisoning recurrences that can only be escaped from by a transformation of the imprisoned self. The popular fantasy of liberation into a South Sea paradise therefore serves only to
resuscitate with purity the old barrenness in its compulsive
re-enactments. As for murder in a bath of lysol – that other
deep solace of the Sunday imagination – the act dramatises
the rage that is the reverse of the Hollow Men's impotence,
the passion for revenge asserting itself outrageously in a mind
laid open by the outrageousness of life. We can go further
and suggest that the act is a too drastic endorsement of St
John of the Cross's view that the soul should divest itself of
the love of created things. Responses are not answers; but
they can cause the reader to reflect upon the nature of a possible answer.

In a statement to Nevill Coghill, Eliot observed that the
'governing idea' for him was that of 'rebirth into supernatural
life through a cycle of which the descent into the dark night
of the soul is a recurring preliminary.' This idea 'appeared as
a process' both for the professed mystic and for the common
man whether he recognised it or not and Sweeney was 'the
common man, the average, decent lout.'[2] We have here a
Sweeney some distance from that original apeneck whose
shadow fell across Emerson's view of history. Disgust, or if
we prefer it, the boredom and horror which precede the
glory,[3] seem to have been transferred from the sardonic observer to the consciousness observed, a consciousness which
had previously seemed no more than the destined denizen of
those lithe quatrains. On the 'higher' level it can be pointed
out that Prufrock, Gerontion, and the shadowy mental traveller in the Waste Land are scarcely embodiments of the mystic
consciousness. Yet the 'governing idea' surely gains in potency
when those who carry it forward are not its conscious adhe-
rents. And the individuality of the advance is not to be

slighted. Every dark night in poetry has its own palpability and its own *frisson*, as Eliot's own work suggests to us when we set *The Hollow Men* beside *The Dry Salvages*.

From that initial gesture of journeying in *Prufrock* the ripples of exploration widen and it is the force of the outreaching, the many classes, the several tones of talk, the angular collisions of past and present, the polyglot juxtapositions, the language-landscape denuded of connectives to allow the evidence to be fully itself, the mind searching for its structure in everything that the mind has found significant, that drives us with the full resources of poetry into confrontation of the human impasse. What we witness is not simply a failure which surrounds us completely because it is comic and tragic and epic but the failure of the entire civilizing effort when it chooses to start from the mind as its own place. It is a failure which must be felt out in order to be fought through. East of Eden there is no other beginning.

Eliot's description of his 'governing idea' plots a curve which may be sadly familiar. From the personal disillusionment of Gerontion and Prufrock we move according to the popular interpretation, through the 'disillusionment of a generation' embodied in *The Waste Land*, to the exhausted nadir of *The Hollow Men*, identified helpfully with its last two lines. The numbed soul turns to faith and death's other kingdom consists of the poetry of piety. For more intelligent critics, the hollow men can lack Paul Tillich's courage to be, or are finally damned to 'total paralysis, corresponding for the mind and soul, to the doom forecast by scientists, in accordance with the principle of entropy for our "valley of dying stars." '[4]

It is not certain that the Hollow Men are damned. They stand on the banks of a river which as a later poem tells us, is within us, and which is Dante's river as well as Conrad's. There is no evidence that the river is not crossed except the evidence that the crossing is dreaded. People have been known to successfully undertake what they fear and what they consider themselves incapable of doing. In the language of the borderline, fear and a felt incapacity may well be the preliminary to any forward movement.

We are dealing we must remember, not with a terminal poem that closes a book and calls for a new beginning but with a poem in a continuity, a movement into the terms of understanding that is meticulously sought out and inched through. That movement had left the 'I' of *The Waste Land* with the arid plain behind him, having heard the thunder speak at the horizon of his understanding. The dispositions of the poem left it uncertain whether the imperatives of the thunder were felt as any more authentic than the warnings of, for example, Madame Sosostris. There is tact rather than confusion in this uncertainty. It may well be that the principles by which the self is reconstituted are added in the first place to the débris of the self and that their importance is discerned only by living beside them. These ambivalences can be differently weighed; but however we weigh them, the situation at the end of *The Waste Land* is best described as a limited and tentative break-out rather than a break-through. The mind must first accept what it has seen at its conceptual perimeter and it must then learn to remake itself around what it has accepted. If we may draw on the assistance of a later poem what we have at this stage is something less than 'the hint half-guessed, the gift half-understood.'

No reflection is needed to show that it would be blatantly indecorous for the final figure of *The Waste Land* to advance, giving, sympathising, and controlling, triumphantly into the sunrise of meaning. An advance respectably restrained would also simplify the state of life on the border, the paralysis that can lie between a past imprisoning one in its known futility and a future terrifying in its openness. *The Hollow Men*, let us add, does not insist upon the universality of this paralysis. There are those who have already crossed the river 'with direct eyes,' there are the violent damned whose tradition Sweeney inherits, and there are those connoisseurs of chaos led by Kurtz, of whom Gerontion is the enfeebled representative. The Hollow Men can stand among these other examples, not without accuracy for the clerisy,[5] for the best who lack conviction, for habits of mind which once commanded thought, reduced to the triviality of a habitual shuffle. To suggest this is not, one hopes, to make a restrictive identification – there are few among us whom the poem does not re-proach – but rather to help in pointing to the poem's locus on the map of our voyaging.

Some corroboration of this locus is provided by the use of an epigraph from *Heart of Darkness* for *The Hollow Men*, instead of as originally planned for *The Waste Land*, and the taking of the epigraph from a later point in Conrad's influential tale. We know that Pound doubted if Conrad was 'weighty enough to stand the citation' and that Eliot defended the deleted *Waste Land* epigraph as 'somewhat elucidative' and 'much the most appropriate' he could find.[6] It is not unusual to infer that Eliot acquiesced in the deletion because of Pound's disapproval and, on a larger scale, to conclude that the overall 'statement' of Eliot's earlier work might have been better framed without the benefit of Pound's management. Russell Kirk conjectures for instance that if Eliot had not yielded to Pound's energy we might have had: 'the Great Refusal of Gerontion, followed by the delineation of sterility in *The Waste Land*, and incorporating the picture of the Hollow Men's vacuity – altogether, with transitional and elucidatory passages, a more coherent denunciation of modern disorder, more fully representative of Eliot's own intellect and method.'[7]

For many of us it is the sparseness of 'transitional and elucidatory passages' which brings before us with bleak directness and astringent authenticity that 'modern disorder' which another poet was to describe as the 'desolation of reality.'[8] Certainly no 'method' better conveys the effort of the experiencing self to know the phenomena of which it is both interpreter and victim, the entanglements it must identify and work through in order to discern what principles are clutched by the roots growing beneath the stony rubbish. As for the Hollow Men, we can argue that it is not vacuous to be overcome by an intense and encircling sense of one's own futility. We are at a low point in the experiencing movement – five o'clock in the morning is the locus in time – but the subtleties of poetry can and do convey the tenuous genesis of a counter-movement marked by (and for some critics unfortunately masked by) the degree of meaninglessness to which the poem has brought us.

The new epigraph from *Heart of Darkness* is not simply an affirmation of Eliot's stubborn faith in Conrad's weightiness. In *The Waste Land* the Sybil wanted to die, weary perhaps of foreseeing the eternal recurrence. In *The Hollow Men* Kurtz is dead, bonfires will consume the straw self from which one seeks liberation, and the chain of recurrence need no longer be binding. It is important that in one of the poem's early gestures, its territory is looked back on in remembrance by those who have already crossed the river. The Hollow Men are not free of the world on the banks of which they cluster but in an important sense it is behind them. So it is the 'dead land,' a place of 'broken stone,' a 'valley of dying stars,' a 'broken jaw' of a 'lost kingdom' which we can think of not too fancifully, as excavated in the future from the archaeological memory. The poem's world is in addition 'death's dream kingdom,' a place of hollowness but also of protective illusion, the last defence against dying into reality.

That there are consistent discriminations between death's dream kingdom, death's twilight kingdom, and death's other kingdom is evident, but the speaker poised between memory and desire, the hold of illusion and the fear of renewal, responds to those discriminations in different ways. There can be relief that the eyes that mirror reality are not met even in dreams in death's dream kingdom. There is also the knowledge that one is sightless without the consciousness of what those eyes see. Hieronimo's mad again and the conspirators, wearing disguises, speak in whispers as they plan their escape. Later in the poem they avoid speech. If the silence comments on what lies behind, it also responds to what lies ahead. The world the Hollow Men seek to leave may be empty of meaning but the potentially meaningful is by definition dangerous. The demand of life is that one surrender an identity to which the instinct clings, though the intellect knows it to be hollow. The shadow falls at the point where the commitment has been made but the act of relinquishment still has to be lived through by a mind that is 'terrified and cannot surrender.'

Since the poem's actors in the words of *Burnt Norton*, inhabit a 'place of disaffection,' of 'tumid apathy' beside a tumid river, their sense of death's three kingdoms reflects the shifting equilibrium of the divergent pulls in their nature. The 'dream kingdom,' as the epithet suggests, is a place of defensive illusion. The 'other kingdom,' distanced by the word chosen, is also separate in its nature, an otherness of reality, but belonging to death in the sense that one must shed the self of illusion in order to gain access to it. Though described unavoidably in the imagery of obsolescent experience (the fading star and the broken column), it is a point of transformation that lies beyond that experience. The 'twilight kingdom,' to use the language of *Ash-Wednesday*, is 'the time of tension between dying and birth,' the 'place of solitude where three dreams cross' (the relationship with *The Hollow Men*'s three kingdoms seems instructive) and 'the dream-crossed twilight between birth and dying.' It is in this kingdom that we may be permitted our first sight of the multifoliate rose.

To a writer so creatively steeped in Dante, whose work is ushered in by a quotation from *The Inferno* and who returns to the source in every major poem except *Gerontion*, the first appearance of the rose is surely crucial. It should modify the view so often tritely advanced that *The Hollow Men* is an unredeemed dance of futility. We do not need to react from this finding by declaring the poem an essay in optimism. It should be sufficient to note that the many critics who describe the predicament of the Hollow Men fail to observe that it is to the Hollow Men themselves that they owe the telling accuracy of their descriptions. This self-awareness of the protagonists should be an important and possibly the most important element in our assessment of those minute but crucial increments of advance that orient the movement being made in the direction of meaning. Though futility is not redeemed by the intense consciousness of futility, there can be no hope of redeeming it without this initial recognition. Moreover, what is involved is not simply the repetitive shuffle of the meaningless but the failure of the will to detach itself from an identity the mind knows to be obsolete. The will's helplessness in the face of the demand for life is the core of a crisis which many minds have encountered, but the crisis is put here in representative terms, in terms which are uniquely the language of their century, and in terms which the momentum of

Eliot's poetic effort has slowly brought forward to the present conclusion. It is only when the diagnosis has worked down to this depth that the edge of the mind receives the possibility of entering, not the country of the rose, but at least a territory which reflects its presence.

The thunder calls on us to give, to sympathize, and to achieve control through an act of commitment which is experienced as a surrender of control. The movement from *The Waste Land* to *The Hollow Men* is apparent in the siting of the latter poem (on the river bank before the imminent crossing), in the progress of disintegration (the waste land crumbling into the broken land), in the counter-movement of self-understanding, and in the shadowy but still real awareness of a different world across the river within us. It is a movement profoundly registered in one of the most moving moments in Eliot's poetry, when the injunction to give and to sympathize seems to have been translated into existence and the reaching out 'trembling with tenderness' results only in 'prayers to broken stone.' We have to link this defeat to the later recognition that the perpetual star and the multifoliate rose can be the hope only of 'empty men.' The epithet is fastidiously chosen. There is a difference between hollowness and emptiness, which puts the former on the road to the latter, but only given the continuing effort to cleanse 'affection from the temporal.' Once again we confront St John of the Cross's requirement that the soul should divest itself of the love of created things. But we encounter it in circumstances that call for a reconciliation with the thunder's injunction to give and to sympathize. A doctrinal reconciliation can be outlined but what we are contemplating is a poetic document of the human journey and that document at this stage in its honesty can only record the depth of frustration and attempt to move forward to the understanding that the mind must be empty of needs and expectations if the shape of things is to be inscribed upon it. If there is a reconciliation between the human and the demanded it must be symbolic rather than doctrinal. The multifoliate rose is such a consolation, a symbol that is equally responsive to the hunger for design and the cry for natural fulfillment.

The Hollow Men is concerned with the distance of dread between essence and existence, between what is conceptually known and what must consequently be abandoned, not just intellectually but by every resource of the whole man. The shadow falls with ominous and cumulative force across seven different renderings of this distance. Dowson fathered the phrase and Shakespeare's *Julius Caesar* is remembered,[9] but given the observations which are usually made about *The Hollow Men* we should in addition pay attention to Eliot's remark, apropos of Baudelaire, that there is a difference between hysteria and looking into the shadow.[10] The whole passage underlines this difference, moving with dexterity across the poem's natural ambivalences. The shadow is the shadow of death. It falls across the passage from one of death's kingdoms to another. It can be thought of as barring the passage. It can also be thought of as necessary to that transit. 'For thine is the kingdom' takes on a certain colouration in the poem since all three kingdoms are felt to be death's kingdoms by a consciousness preparing to die into life. Even in the terms chosen to annotate the distance between what is known and willed and its 'embodiment,' we have the shadow falling between the desire and the spasm and between potency and existence. The spasm can be the spasm of death or the spasm of the generation of life. Both enter into and by their co-presence define the transvaluation that takes place as we achieve the crossing of the river within ourselves.

The penultimate stanza faithfully enacts the struggle that characterises the poem. Within the overall orchestration it achieves the necessary diminuendo, the stuttering before the final whimper. But the contending principles of 'For Thine is the kingdom' and 'life is very long' are also pared down to their essential states, abbreviated to take on the finality of the word 'is.' When the superior principle takes on an extra syllable something has been gained in the micro-drama. We can begin to think of the possibility of the full proposition entering the whole mind. It is a dramatic renewal of the tactics of the closing of *The Waste Land*. The helpless mumble contains the small seed of significance.

The first temptation of the writer is to see artistic form as a means of deliverance from the actual. As the inescapability of the actual asserts itself, form becomes a means of grappling with and controlling its brute force, of transmuting it into purified and cardinal relationships. 'The immense panorama of futility and anarchy which is contemporary history' is given coherence by the mythical method. Writing elsewhere of Joyce, Eliot tells us that 'what is needed of art is the simplification of current life into something rich and strange.' He goes on to say that 'the craving for the fantastic, for the strange, is legitimate and perpetual; everyone with a sense of beauty has it. The strongest, like Mr Joyce, make their feeling into an articulate external world.'[11] It is clear that even in this year before *The Waste Land*, the singing of Prufrock's mermaids haunted Eliot. It is also clear that the experience of *The Waste Land* moved him beyond that singing. Nevertheless in the lecture on Arnold several years later, the pursuit of Beauty is still under way and what is to be achieved is a true sense of 'glory' even though it can only be achieved by accepting and enduring the 'boredom and the horror.'[12] We can take these remarks as expressing the relationship of the Hollow Men to the multifoliate rose but the connection would not sound the depths of the poem. It is to the essay on Pascal that we must turn once again for a more searching formulation. Here the 'end of all our exploring' is not beauty but peace, and peace found not through submission to dogma, but through 'a satisfaction of the whole being.' The special problem for which Pascal serves as mentor is the achieving of that peace by the intelligence committed to scepticism but yearning for design, by 'those who doubt, but who have the mind to conceive, and the sensibility to feel, the disorder, the futility, the meaninglessness, the mystery of life and suffering.'[13] *The Hollow Men* can be thought of as a poem which lies unavoidably on the road of such a mind, a poem numbingly aware of the futile and the meaningless in the death dance of the illusion which we term life, but also a poem which seeks the outskirts of the mystery through the distant presence of the rose and the star.

II

Though the four Ariel poems appear in *Collected Poems* after *Ash-Wednesday*, they were originally published on both sides of that poem. A chronological consideration has its advantages – *Marina* in particular belongs to a world only made possible by *Ash-Wednesday* – but there are also rewards in examining the poems as a group. Apart from *Marina*, the most radiant poem that Eliot wrote, the Ariel sequence does not crucially advance the language of comprehension but the poems are by no means five-finger exercises. Published in successive Decembers, they can be regarded as a Nativity grouping: two poems respond to the divine birth, a third considers human birth as the beginning of our dying, and the fourth moves forward to rebirth and reinstatement within a lost reality. It is not suggested that the four poems should be hammered relentlessly into this frame but the frame will suffice as an initial statement of their cogency.

The Hollow Men huddle together on the bank of a river, separating illusion from the possibility of attaining reality. The Magi have crossed the mountains, visited another country, and been witness to a transforming event. It cannot be said that they are overcome by the enlightenment of the word about to be spoken, or by the tragedy of the word to be betrayed. Their grouchy realism strikes a new note which can be contrasted, for instance, with Yeats's 'pale, unsatisfied' figures, arresting the moment in their own carved immobility.[14] Beginning in a neat deflection of the words of Lancelot Andrewes,[15] the language, not to mention the mountain journey, looks forward to Auden and to others. It also reminds us that the word is not heard only by those who are involved demandingly in the struggle to hear it by the very nature of the poetic or religious enterprise.

The journey the Magi make foreshadows the crucifixion in what is seen en route, while taking in an image which Eliot singles out as 'charged with emotion' for him.[16] Thus the wise men move through the future on their way to the timeless. Reporting the journey with verisimilitude rather than understanding, they 'set down' the question which the journey raises. Othello's phrase, doubling upon itself, directs us to an ambiguous summing-up. The Birth was 'hard and bitter agony' for those who watched it self-centredly and 'like Death, our death' for the citizens of illusion. Yet something was born in those less than enthusiastic witnesses. What was born was possibly a readiness to die. The return home is a return to exile, to an alien people clutching outmoded gods. The final line opens itself to more than one reading: the death of the 'old dispensation,' the renewed presence of the birth which calls for death, the death on the cross, and the taking over of the mind by a significance which has so far been witnessed rather than known.

The Magi can acknowledge the need for something like death because of an event beyond and within themselves that has left them 'no longer at ease' in the status quo. If Simeon responds to the Nativity by wishing for death, it is for reasons that differ from those of the Magi or for that matter the Sybil. Comparisons with Gerontion are not entirely useful. With 'eighty years and no to-morrow' Simeon may belong to Gerontion's age group but his inadequacy does not lie in his past or in that world the profit of which Gerontion sought to protract. The hyacinths, Eliot's flowers of illusion, bloom in the poem but they bloom in bowls and Simeon does not share in their transient life. On the other hand he does not turn to the new life of which he is a witness or commit himself to the conclusion, shaped in a later Eliot poem, that 'old men ought to be explorers.' Gerontion feared Christ the tiger. Simeon's fear is of the tigers of history, the rending cost of achieving the word in the world. Just and devout as the source in Luke indicates,[17] he has observed his obligations, provided for the poor, lived out his season, and deserved his exit. His unpreparedness to take part in what he foresees can be judged with appropriate severity but what he foresees is surely a telling commentary on the wish of the Magi for another death. In addition, it puts before us a matter which is to become more prominent in Eliot's poetic and dramatic thought, namely the place of vision in an ordinary world. Not all of us can pay the price demanded of Celia Coplestone. Is a life devoid of all significance the only alternative to a life resolutely centred on significance? Is there no middle ground

for 'most of us' between that 'occupation for the saint' for
which Simeon is clearly unready and a world apprehended
over the tinkle of coffee spoons, or the sturdier rhythms of
birth, copulation, and death? These considerations make it
difficult to talk easily of Simeon's 'failure.' The poem is better seen as a further enlargement in our understanding of the
mixed character of the twilight kingdom.

If the response to authentic life is the wish for death, un-
authentic life is the wrong kind of dying. That we begin to
die from the moment we are born is the proposition behind
Animula, given weight by the studied contrast between the
simple soul issuing from the hand of God and the misshapen
soul issuing from the hand of time, by the violent climactic
images of the poem, and by the twist given the last line. Yet
the development of the poem is less relentless than this outline suggests. We are not really dealing with a seed of destructiveness planted within the soul which time and experience
bring to its disastrous fruition, though it is clear that some
continuity is intended between the poem's initial images of
frustration and its final images of calamitous self-will. Nevertheless the centre of attention is the collision between the
mind and the world, between creative curiosity and the baf-
fling, obstinate givenness of the actual. Moving on from its
source in *Purgatorio* XVI, which Eliot quotes in his essay on
Dante,[18] the poem examines the tension between the golden
world and the brazen, between 'the actual and the fanciful,'
between what 'the fairies do and what the servants say.' The
verbal pattern nicely relates the fairies to the 'actual' and
doing is of course more substantial than saying. As tension
deteriorates into conflict, 'desire' confronts 'control,' and the
'pain of living' becomes the alternative to an imaginative
world now no more than the 'drug of dreams.' The balances
of the line remember the eighteenth century but what is said
recalls the fifth stanza of *Among School Children* and that
'ignominy of boyhood' affirmed so eloquently in the *Dialogue of Self and Soul.*[19]

Despite the poem's final images, its main rendition is of
the soul's helplessness. It is 'lame' and 'irresolute,' unable to
fare forward (a phrase nobly annotated by *The Dry Salvages*)

or to retreat to an Eden of simplicity, made uninhabitable by collision with the world. In 'denying the importunity of the blood,' its failure to commit itself reminds us of 'blood shaking the heart' in the thunder's elaboration of its first imperative. It follows that 'control' should be felt as repressive rather than as the free declaration of the fulfilled soul. Here and elsewhere the poem joins itself to Eliot's world, though it is scarcely, as one critic finds it, important enough to form an introduction to that world.[20] It does not fully succeed in bridging the distance between its beginning and its end. To put it differently, it does not completely deliver us from the hope that the human condition can be rectified by a more adequate knowledge of child psychology.

The poem ends with Eliot's version of the epic catalogue, a swirl of menace that recalls *Gerontion* in the evocative force of its naming. Though Grover Smith objects to Boudin on the ground that 'as a common noun it generally means black pudding,'[21] the infelicity should merely remind us that a poem does not always attract into its range of connotation everything that a word has been in its history. The dominant tone should form the field of force and persuade us to the necessary exclusions. In this particular listing the combination of the representative and anonymous (the ones who made great fortunes and who went their own way) with the individual disaster summoned arrestingly from the poetic memory point to an end both universal and inescapably personal. The final naming is powerfully symbolic. That Actaeon should be remembered is natural and a connection with the Hound of the Baskervilles is faintly possible though entirely unnecessary.[22] More important is the planting of those yew trees which are to become dominant symbols in Eliot's poetic universe. It is surely deliberate that Floret is slain between them. In *Ash-Wednesday* the silent sister is between the same yews and is besought to pray for those who are 'terrified and cannot surrender.' The yew trees are emblems of death and resurrection presiding over 'the life of significant soil.' Between them we have the end or the beginning, violent death or creative intercession, the hunter brought down in the importunity of the blood, or that deeper importunity to which the blood contributes, the cry of the whole man for significance, which the silent sister guides towards an answer. The climactic event can be either obliterating or originating. 'Pray for us now and at the hour of our birth' has more than one meaning when it is read between the yews.

Marina, the last of the Ariel poems, places itself between the yew trees through the relationship between its title and its epigraph. The epigraph from Seneca recalls an incident in which Hercules, having killed his children in a fit of madness, awakes to reality in a landscape which we can think of as made foreign by the alienating force of his own destructiveness. The analogy with original sin is obvious. Eliot may conceivably have been unaware of the tradition of christianizing Hercules but both the epigraph and the fourth section of *Little Gidding* attach themselves effectively to this tradition. If death is one yew, renewal is the other. In taking his title from Shakespeare's *Pericles* Eliot puts it to us that we can recover as well as discover what has been lost. It is of course not only the title but the radiance of the poem which is late Shakespearean[23] just as the dark congestion of *Gerontion* recreates that more sombre world of Shakespeare from which the earlier poem takes its epigraph. In paralleling his movement with that of a 'dead master' Eliot suggests not only the line of his advance but those continuities of concern which are the true history of poetry.

Precisely because the epigraph and the title engage each other in so evocative a relationship, we should refrain from making them points of reference in an expository diagram. Shakespeare does not parallel or even run at right angles to Seneca. Marina is not killed, though she is exposed to the kind of fate that is usually described as worse than death and is saved from it only by her disconcerting goodness. Her misfortunes, in any event, are attributable to no fault of her father. Moreover, she is found eventually by the peripatetic Pericles, while the voyager in Eliot gropes onward, guided by what some critics allege is the deception of the thrush in Prufrock's fog. The tone of the poem can scarcely sustain so bitterly ironic a reading. The fog is surely meant to be penetrated, not wrapped protectively round the quiescent self. If the thrush deceives the children of *Burnt Norton*, another thrush singing in the pine trees is the sign of life for which the traveller in the Waste Land thirsts. The interplay of epigraph and title indicates that as we re-enact the madness of Hercules we stop short of the obliteration of the future. But goodness, even though and perhaps because it is blameless, is exposed to the onslaught of the world's cruelty, as it is most mercilessly in *King Lear*. The reconciliation with creativeness can come only with guidance from a source beyond ourselves and only at a frontier sufficiently remote to make bleakly evident the range of our destructiveness. This is how the conflation presumably works for Eliot and if it is debatable as a reading of *Pericles* we must remember that we are looking at a creative response to Shakespeare rather than at an exercise in Shakespearean criticism.

The mythic foundation of *Marina* and indeed of Eliot's œuvre, his macro-poem of the human journey, is the passage beyond India to a lost paradise, the discovery at the frontier, of the source. Because we 'arrive where we started,' the most remote is also the immediate, 'more distant than stars and nearer than the eye.' Because the exploration is the searching of the mind as well as the mind searching, the outer horizon is the inmost depth, 'under sleep where all the waters meet.' The ship of the self, battered by inclemencies, 'cracked with ice' and also 'cracked with heat,' with its rigging weak and its canvas rotten, nevertheless seeks its creative principle, driven forward by the memory of its magnetic north, that shaping force of which it was once the vessel. The garboard strake that leaks, taken from a rejected section of *The Waste Land*,[24] underlines Eliot's insistent preoccupation with the voyage of the self into the strange seas of self-knowledge. Even the language in its evolutions of sound shaping evolutions of meaning ('unknowing, half-conscious, unknown, my own'), suggests how we have 'forgotten/And remember,' how at the outer limits, we can glimpse the constant core.

We can now return to the question of why Marina is not found. Pericles hears the music of the spheres. The point of intersection, which may be taken as a post-Newtonian equivalent to Pythagoras, does not enter Eliot's poetry until well after *Marina*. But the reason is not simply that other poems need to be written or that conclusive and joyous discovery is foreign to Eliot's fastidious moderation. We are too far advanced in the distancings of culture and the erosions of self-consciousness for finality to be part of the modern vision. The purpose of a destination in our time is not to offer a resting place but to equip the mind for a new voyage. The solid rhythms of destructiveness in *Marina* can 'dissolve' and become 'insubstantial' as the dominant gives way to the real. The evanescent rhythms of life can become clearer and stronger. Yet these rhythms retain their characteristic fragility, underlining our awareness that the new life, for which the old life is resigned, is offered in 'a world of time' with the poem carefully distanced from the threshold of that offer. As if to suggest the nature of that threshold, speech is given up for the unspoken word; for the lips parted to speak, for the awakening, the hope,' and finally for the 'new ships.' To fare forward remains the creative injunction. We shall not cease from exploration but it is not true that there is no end but addition.

CHAPTER FOUR

The Time of the Tension

For many readers *Ash-Wednesday* still marks a decisive turn in Eliot's poetry and for some of them it is still a turn for the worse. The sceptical intelligence becomes the conforming mentality. The satirist looking down at the bleak geometry of the human predicament becomes the transcendentalist looking upwards for intimations of the eternal pattern. *The Waste Land* put before us an archetypal desert in which any text of salvation could be preached. Eliot not only chose the wrong text; he chose a traditional text to follow a revolutionary poem.

These statements should be profoundly unsatisfying to those who have followed the progress of Eliot's poetry, the scrupulously earned advance into understanding, with each stage negotiated in an act of language fitted to it and laying bare its nature. From the beginning the work has been aware of the narrow passage from illusion to reality, evaded by Prufrock, contemplated with terror by Gerontion, approached in *The Waste Land* to an extent making possible the announcements of the thunder, numbly awaited in *The Hollow Men*, and recounted in the *Magi* as an uncomfortable excursion rather than an experience. From the beginning we have also advanced through a series of stylistic deployments making it evident that the mind moves forward only by finding and authenticating the language which makes possible forward movement: Laforguean irony, Jacobean rhetoric, the prehensile energy of the Sweeney quatrains, the polyglot, densely allusive geology of *The Waste Land*, the radiant yet tentative reshapings of *Marina* are among the applications of the inventiveness and the relatedness, the uses of the past in defining the destitutions of the present. The whole resolute movement is original rather than revolutionary, radical in the sense of persistently seeking its roots. *The Waste Land*, which may seem a conspicuous exception can, in fact, be treated as a highly conservative poem. Indeed, when it is read in conjunction with 'Tradition and the Individual Talent' Eliot would seem to be implying that the only way to write a traditional poem at that point in his century was to write it with a violently experimental surface.

Reference has been made to the sceptical intelligence and perhaps we should consider the proposition, potent in the academic world, that all intelligence is sceptical. Eliot honours this proposition for what it is worth and it is not worth everything. He cannot, in the end, co-operate with the view that the only text that can be preached in the waste land is the text claiming that no text is possible. His is the classic relationship between scepticism and faith, exemplified for instance by Sir Thomas Browne, though Eliot reaches his settlement through an advance far more protracted and exacting than any set down by the urbane doctor from Norfolk. If the meaninglessness eventually guides Eliot to the mystery, the understanding must be achieved and not announced; the voice of the thunder signifies only the terms of further exploration. And the settlement when reached cannot endure. Time in its corrosive nature demands the renewal of any conclusion that is achieved in time. It is not merely *Marina* and the concluding section of *Ash-Wednesday* but the entire movement of *Four Quartets* which make it clear that there can be no harbour and no garden except to equip the mind for a new exile.

The first section of *Ash-Wednesday* turns with a sometimes wry resignation on the double possibilities of turning – into illusion, or from illusion to reality. To make possible the turn for the better, one must not only avoid those attachments that give the turn into illusion impetus, but make sure that those attachments are not reborn as motive forces in the turn to what seems reality. What is required is not the transference of energies to a superior objective but the renunciation of energies in order that the objective can be recognized. The state to be reached is a kind of higher aimlessness. Beginning with a quotation from Cavalcanti and continuing with one from Shakespeare to which a slight change is made,[1] Eliot proceeds to ring all possible changes on his negative incantation. The language is psychologically just in conveying a central inertia and the apparently mindless activity of the mind in that inertia; but closer examination shows, as F.R. Leavis has tellingly shown us, that the variations are intelligently controlled rather than randomly shuffled.[2] 'I no longer strive to strive towards such things,' for instance, enacts through the repetition and the strenuous distancing, the potentially self-defeating effort which the mind must make to remove itself adequately from effort. The following line has irritated those who believe as Edmund Wilson did that life begins at forty.[3] But the point is that even the poetic aspiration, the eagle's flight towards the sun on which it unflinchingly gazes (Yeats refers to 'the lidless eye that loves the sun'),[4] must be relinquished. It is a prior orientation of an area which has to be emptied. Self-centredness is not simply surrendered to be replaced immediately by god-centredness. Many stages intervene, including an interim without a centre in which the mind must resist any tendency to centre itself. It is in a climactic effort at resistance that the 'blessèd face' and the 'voice' are renounced, both as themselves and as metaphors for a higher commitment. As *The Dry Salvages* will remind us, the most reliable is the fittest for renunciation. Nevertheless the nature of the mind, however scrupulously emptied, is to seek a basis for itself. A poem does more, involving itself unavoidably in acts of orientation, even in seeking to delineate a state that is fully non-oriented. In its grasp of this

paradox and in its embodiment of it, Eliot's language is able
to bring out, far more effectively than the mystical traditions
by which he is so strongly influenced, the mind's propensity
to populate an emptiness in the very acts by which that
emptiness is created. It is this awareness which makes the
poet's prayer that he may forget matters that he has discussed
too much with himself and explained too much to himself
more than the weary dismissal of the mind's directionless
activity. The surface permutations are part of the way in
which the experience is felt. But the experience means more
in its potentialities and betrayals and a highly controlled act
of language is necessary to keep that meaning in being. The
later 'teach us to care and not to care' summarizes a state already made intensely real by the difficulty of reaching it. To
'sit still' involves wise passivity, unrelaxing watchfulness,
without reaching out and without self-orientation, a withdrawal of the mind from its natural functions that maintains
intact its integrity as mind. But whatever its future implications, the aimlessness of the state must be felt and accepted
and while it is felt, the aimlessness will be real and not apparent. The eagle's wings are vans, beating an air so rarefied that
it no longer supports the notion of flight.

The second section of *Ash-Wednesday* was originally entitled 'Salutation,' recalling Dante's encounter with Beatrice
in the *Vita Nuova* after 'nine years were exactly completed.'
A deleted epigraph quoted Dante's words to Bonagiunta de
Lucca (*Purgatorio* XXIV) in describing his 'dolce stil novo.'
The rest of the epigraph consisted of a quotation from Ezekiel 37.[5] Though these associations remain important, their
deletion means that we confront in their immediacy the three
white leopards (however tranquilly recollected) and the remains which they devour. It is possible to identify these leopards with the world, the flesh, and the devil (or with any
other promising triad)[6] and to note that they feed collec-
tively or better still respectively, on the traditional loci of
the natural, vital, and animal spirits. The two triads can then
be linked to three forms of renunciation in the first section of
Ash-Wednesday if doing so gives satisfaction to the reader.[7]
Some may not think that this is a necessary consequence of

Yeats's view that 'all ancient vision was definite and precise.'[8] Precision does not mean that every term in a vision must have a precise equivalence. It does mean that everything seen should be seen unambiguously in the frame of its own world, however ambiguous or evocative it may be in translation. Indeed ambiguity and evocativeness may be the cost of any translation, a measure of the distance between the vision and 'actuality.'

The section is certainly in a sweet new style, all the more remarkable because of the events it narrates. Nine years will serve to indicate the trials of the passage from 'living and partly living' into life. The leopards who devour the poet-prophet under a juniper tree taken from I Kings 19 and from Grimm's story of that title[9] destroy the old self and allow the new to be created from its unpromising remnants. Ezekiel 37 to which some of the lines in this section allude, is a testimony to this creative power. It is a power made available by the 'goodness' of the 'Lady of Silences' who can be thought of as a higher version of that lady whose blessèd face and voice were earlier renounced. But the dissembled self seeks not resurrection but oblivion, and though it is this wish which ensures its survival, it still seeks to be forgotten and to forget. The dry bones which, as *The Waste Land* observes, 'can harm no one,' are invited to prophesy to the winds, not to carry God's message to the four corners of the earth, but because only the wind will listen to their prophecy. They sing chirping with the burden of the grasshopper (an ironic echo of Ecclesiastes 12:5) instead of proclaiming the power of God. The translucent verse lets us see through to the serenity of the occasion, the inconsequentiality of action past and future, the happiness of being 'devoted, concentrated in purpose,' however trivial the elements that enter the act of devotion.

The song of the dry bones has been described as a litany of paradoxes but while it is certainly that, it is also more. The paradoxes convey the nature of the lady as it is beyond time, and as it becomes in its involvement with time, her nature as it is, and her nature as it responds to the anguished act of reaching out to that nature. And if the single rose is now the garden, it is because individual experience has been placed in a general meaning. If love satisfied is a greater torment than unsatisfied love, it is because it calls us to responsibility, because it demands that we carry the purity of vision into the corruptions of the world. If all that is inconclusible is brought to a conclusion, that may finally mean that we are allowed to see where the end lies so that we can be committed to the endeavour to seek it. In the distance between the terms of its paradoxes and its sense of a still point where the distance narrows to nothing, the poetry affirms the discontinuity between eternity and time. The consequence can only be the stubborn resumption of the journey for those whom the gift of life has committed to time's element.

After the bones have completed their litany of devotion, they conclude with a tranquilly ironic coda. Scattered but shining, forgetting themselves and each other, they speak of a condition beyond the dissociated mind and its attempt to work back to its unity from its fragments. The 'cool of the day' recalls the original garden and the price paid to make possible its regaining. The blessing of sand is that it obliterates the past and the otherwise inescapable ravages of 'what is done, not to be done again.' 'This is the land. We have our inheritance' sets in order and carries forward a phrase from *The Waste Land* but also puts it to us that the centre of what we inherit is not the achievement of culture or even the tribute of culture to a world beyond culture, that 'inexplicable splendour' held by the walls of Magnus Martyr. As the creative destitution of the desert strips away the inessential and the consequential, we can see more clearly the heart of our inheritance.

The passage through death has not come easily in Eliot's poetry and the road to the right dying is marked by various simulations. 'Fled is that music. Do I wake or sleep?' is Keats's concluding question in the *Ode to a Nightingale* and Prufrock waking from dream-reality to life-illusion sees himself killed by the sound of human voices. Gerontion, unable to be absolute for death, looks into the void with the terror shown by Claudio in *Measure for Measure*. Phlebas suffers annihilation by drowning, in a grim reminder of man's mortality. The Hollow Men, in a world dominated by death, await what for them can only be felt as the passage from one of death's kingdoms to another. Floret is slain on the threshold of the alternative. In gathering up these simulations and half-misunderstandings, the second section of *Ash-Wednesday* explores and becomes entitled to occupy a place which is not just the result of a change in belief, but which has been created and the tenancy of which is now demanded by the cumulative forward movement of the poetry. The experience of passage is made meaningful and potent for the future of Eliot's work through the step-by-step, ground-level, documented advance, the growth of the mind to the point where passage is possible.

The locus of allusion of *Ash-Wednesday* is clearly cantos XXIV to XXX of the *Purgatorio*. It is, as we have noted, in canto XXIV that Dante encounters Bonagiunta de Lucca. When Dante explains to the earlier poet that fidelity to love's dictation is the animating principle of the new style, we can permit ourselves to see the later Eliot addressing the earlier. Bonagiunta's reply that this difference was all that made him less than Dante has nice reverberations if the parallel is admitted. But this is not the only connection between Eliot's poem and those purgatorial cornices. On the same sixth cornice where Bonagiunta is encountered are two trees, one life-giving but forbidden and the other death-dealing, growing from the same roots as the tree the fruit of which was eaten by Adam and Eve. Perhaps the origin of Eliot's two yew trees is to be found here. On the seventh cornice Dante meets Arnaut Daniel and Arnaut's final words provide a deleted title for what is now the third section of *Ash-Wednesday* as well as a phrase for the fourth section. Beyond the fire which the Provençal poet enters lie the limits of Virgil's mandate and the earthly paradise to which the garden in the fourth section of *Ash-Wednesday* is related. On the banks of Lethe, Dante witnesses a pageant of the church triumphant, which the gilded hearse and jewelled unicorns of *Ash-Wednesday* seem to parody.[10]

Since the garden lies at the summit of the purgatorial ascent and since the analogue to the refining fire is the death by devouring in the second section of *Ash-Wednesday*, it becomes persuasive to argue that the psychic sequence differs from the narrative. Both the second and third sections are related in the past tense and it can be suggested that the first describes a vision and the second the initial stages of the struggle necessary to attain that vision. We can admit this and yet feel that the narrative order has a point to make. The stairway will be climbed more than once in Eliot's poetry and Arnaut Daniel will again enter the fire. Indeed we can argue that the new self is no self until it performs its resurrected nature and that the ascent of the stairway is meant not only to show the new identity being established but also to remind us of the continuing contention by which that identity is held against the world.

The scenes on the stairway are described with a particularity that has invited some to look for sources but the details are surely necessary if the encounters are to be felt as real. The climber looks down upon two earlier crises but the shape struggling with the devil of the stairs at the first turning is the 'same shape' as another in a previous situation, not described. It struggles with the devil of the stairs and is left struggling as the climber looks down on the darkness he subsequently passed through. The 'toothed gullet' of the 'agèd shark' and the 'old man's mouth drivelling, beyond repair' suggest the shedding of the previous self, left below to its contention with the devil. But if this is so then it is the new self which must face the next temptation. The scene is as pictorial as the other two but the artist is of the school of Burne-Jones rather than of Dante.[11] No less significant than the change of styling is the climactic place given to the temptation of the senses. Such a temptation corresponds to the invitation to the banquet in *Paradise Regained* and can be expected to come early in temptation sequences, as it does in Becket's four trials. Power calls to the man of the world and for the intellectual, as Milton well knew, Athens is the deepest distraction. Sensuality may be Samson's snare but one is not normally inclined to think of it as a fatal failing of the Eliot hero. Nevertheless the pull of the natural world is felt with extraordinary strength in the sixth section of *Ash-Wednesday* and this purgation prepares us for the responding force of that pull. *Four Quartets* will go on to show how the natural world is capable of yielding its sudden illuminations as well as its betrayals. We can then appreciate the careful artifice in the styling of this temptation, a wan equivalent of the Bower of Bliss. It is a wanness which is underlined by the sexual flourish with which the scene is introduced. As the symbolically framed scene passes into the response to it, we can also note how 'Blown hair is sweet, brown hair over the mouth blown' reflects both the cadence of the flute and the agitation of the watcher and how the relationship of sound between 'brown' and 'blown' graduates into the euphonic evolution from 'stops' to 'steps.' 'Stops' picks up the previous play by suggesting both the performance on the flute and the hesitation of the climber. 'Distraction' is made more than a notion by the language.

Other relationships declare themselves between the Quartets and the scenes upon the stairway. The struggle with the devil wearing the face of hope and despair leads us to the still point of *Burnt Norton* and to its interior manifestation, the 'inner freedom from the practical desire.' It leads us also through the scene in *East Coker* where the soul is bidden to wait without hope, without love, and finally without thought. 'Lord, I am not worthy' apart from its obvious echoes, points to the finding, once again in *East Coker*, that the wisdom of humility is the only wisdom we can hope to acquire. It is noteworthy that Eliot, who considered Baudelaire 'near to Dante and not without sympathy with Tertullian,' felt that Baudelaire came to attain 'the greatest the most difficult, of the Christian virtues, the virtue of humility.' In addition, Baudelaire 'had to discover Christianity'[12] and it can be suggested that a resolutely poetic movement of discovery, the establishing through specific acts of language of those powerful and concurrent reasons which authenticate the movement into faith, constitutes the basis of Eliot's 'faring forward.'

Familiar signs undergo an appropriate transformation in the garden of section four. The dangerous blue and green of the broad-backed figure seen through the slotted window become the 'various ranks of varied green' and 'blue of larkspur, blue of Mary's colour.' The distracting flautist is borne away along with other flautists and fiddlers. The dry rock and sand of the desert are made cool and firm. Water bestows its blessing in the strengthened fountains and in the freshened springs. A time which in another manifestation can be the 'time of tension' is here the time between sleep and waking, the place of the higher dream, of the years that partake of duration but that seem nevertheless to exist between time and the timeless. The ancient rhyme is made to live with 'a new verse' in a nice commentary on the author's relationship to his inheritance. A presence moves in the garden, wearing white light 'sheathed about her, folded,' anticipating that still point in *Burnt Norton*, surrounded in our apprehension by 'a grace of sense, a white light still and moving.' The healing force is apparent even in the movement of the verse, the extensive overflows that leave the situation open for renewal, the repetitions that return to and alter previous places.

The restorative power of the language is evident and persistent but vigilance suggests that all is not well in the garden. In using the phrase 'redeeming the time' in *Thoughts after Lambeth*, Eliot refers to the world's experiment 'of attempting to form a civilized but non-Christian mentality,' prophesies the failure of the experiment, and talks of the necessity for preserving the faith 'through the dark ages' before the experiment collapses.[13] It may be unreasonable to attach this context to *Ash-Wednesday* but Eliot's resort to the phrase 'redeeming the time' is infrequent and this may be the only occasion on which he has used it in his essays. To have in the mind the closing words of *Thoughts after Lambeth* is certainly not unhelpful as we contemplate those jewelled unicorns drawing the gilded hearse. This is not a procession of the Church Triumphant except by some strenuous straining of the evidence.[14] But the pageant may well join in one symbolic statement the pride of the world and the funeral of the world's values.

We are still only at the threshold where Floret was slain. The vision is 'unread.' The deceptive flautist has been silenced into statuary, his flute 'breathless' so that the higher music can be heard. The fountain springs up and the bird sings down, to anticipate a meeting of earth and sky, the joining of two worlds in the life of significant soil. But no word is heard from the 'silent sister' who bends her head and signs in a significant discrimination from the parted lips of the face seen in *Marina*. Before the word can be spoken, the dream which is no more than a token of the word must be made real by her intercessive force. Meanwhile the garden god stands as a reminder of the other fate that can befall one between the yew trees. The unicorns and the hearse prefigure the betrayal of the word even before the point is reached at which the word can be spoken. The prophecy to the wind and the thousand whispers which the wind is to shake from the yew may suggest the word in process of formation, or its dissolution into whispers like those in *Gerontion*. One of the trees, we must remember, is a tree of death, and it is the 'other yew' which is presented as life-giving in the final section.

In this setting, the final line of the section is profoundly ironic. 'And after this our exile, show unto us the blessed fruit of thy womb, Jesus' is the sentence in the Salve Regina from which Eliot's fragment is taken.[15] The end of a long night of alienation is sought, the fulfillment of the returned soul in the word revealed. But the abridgement of the quotation and the finality of its placing suggest not simply that an exile is about to end, but that a new one is inexorably on the verge of beginning. Eden can be found but not inhabited. To proclaim the word is also to expose it to subversion. The section to follow does not celebrate the healing force of a superior order, the triumphant dismissal of the darkness by the light as in Milton's ode, *On the Morning of Christ's Nativity*. Rather it laments with overwhelmed virtuosity the destructive entanglement of the word in the world. The ground is already being laid for the renewed separation, the unavoidable drift from the centre of understanding, which is to form the just but painful climax of *Ash-Wednesday*.

The opening lines of the next section were once dismissed by Max Eastman as an oily puddle of emotional noises.[16] Eliot is perhaps unduly fascinated by that sentence in Lancelot Andrewes's Nativity sermon which he remembers repeatedly in his poetry and his language lays itself open to his own celebrated remark that we read Milton first for the sound and then for the sense.[17] But the sound is scarcely that of oily stagnation. Perhaps it is making a virtue of excess to argue that the lines enact the drowning of the word in words. There are deeper forms of betrayal to which we should be attentive. Nevertheless there is drama in the storm of language and there are forces regulating the movement of the storm. The distinctions between the Word and words, between the World and the worldly, between stillness in eternity and stillness (persistence) in duration, are maintained and even defined by the turbulence; and the lines act as a metaphysical prelude to the text from Micah 6 ('Oh my people, what have I done unto thee') which calls the betrayer to penitence. The decorum of the occasion is skilfully used to make clear how the garden is lost even as the garden is attained. The turn becomes all the more decisive when we consider it not simply as crucial in *Ash-Wednesday* but as confronting and threatening to annul a cumulative movement into meaning, the scrupulously achieved, passionately earned advance of the questioning and yet yearning intelligence.

There are other occasions in the calendar which call for rejoicing in the presence of the word, but, with the qualified exception of *Marina*, Eliot refrains from putting them to use. The word is not spoken and neither the right time or the right place are here. The landscape can be varied but neither the peace of islands, the commerce of continents, the barrenness of deserts, nor the fertility of rainlands provide a soil for significance. Intercession can make the soil tillable but even among those who have reached the threshold, intercession encounters both co-operation and terrified resistance within the stony places of the heart. Those not torn to pieces by the boar hound are torn on the horn between the claims of competing orders. Like the soul in *Animula*, they are unable to fare forward or retreat. They will not go away and cannot pray. They oppose what they have chosen; the full rhyme necessitating the past tense is subtle in suggesting how acceptance and rejection are involved with each other and how the commitment is overlaid by the immediacy of the reistance. The progress through the heart's ambivalences comes to a climax in the contrast between affirming before the world (which may be doing the right deed for the wrong reason of vanity) and denying between the rocks when the cost of affirmation cannot be escaped. Yet ambivalence can turn upon itself in a final doubling of paradox, and if there is a desert in the garden, as this section of *Ash-Wednesday* has made evident, there is also a garden in the desert, as the previous section has made tranquilly clear.[18] Paradise and Calvary stand in one place, as Eliot could have learned from a poet who influenced him deeply[19] and according to one tradition a withered seed, placed in Adam's mouth as he lay dying, grew into the tree from which the Cross was made.[20] Both Adams can meet within the nature of man but only when that nature has moved itself forward to the point of meeting through the earnestness and momentum of its own struggle. Yet the moral imagination which urges the mind to this threshold does so by endowing it with a dual capability: if it can apprehend the word it can also betray it.

Ash-Wednesday has moved between striving and peace. The opening effort to achieve passivity, to fully silence the will, to open the mind freely and without previous dispositions to the entry of the higher understanding, is followed by the quietness of rebirth in the desert. The struggle on the stairway gives access to the order and sweetness of the garden. It is succeeded by the controlled turbulence of section five, the most profound agitation that the poem has so far undergone. As the last section takes up the opening words of the poem, it becomes evident that this rhythm will not be preserved, that the conclusion is not to be peace but rather a further documentation of the continuing effort which is the human element. The seemingly minor change from 'because' to 'although' and the implication that the sector through which the turn takes place may have altered measure with ironic precision the advance that has been registered. We are invited by the verbal minimization to reflect on the difference between the real and the apparent distance travelled. The next line remembers the death of Phlebas the Phoenician in the higher meaning it gives to profit and loss. The 'dream-crossed twilight' of the line that follows has been typologically anticipated in the 'violet hour' of *The Waste Land* and in the 'twilight kingdom' of *The Hollow Men*. The transit through the twilight is described as brief and the ominousness of that brevity becomes speedily apparent as the poem turns back again to its beginning, with not striving to strive replaced by not wishing to wish. Then the agèd eagle is replaced in its turn by the 'unbroken wings' of the white sails flying seaward. The repetition in 'fly seaward, seaward flying,' the wheeling of the phrase upon its comma, the soaring cadence, and the 'wide window' contrasted with the slotted window of an earlier distraction, dramatically open out the horizons of longing, making decisively real the pull of the natural world.

The lost heart stiffens, with a double meaning given to 'lost' and with 'stiffens' suggesting first awakened alertness and then the wrong direction taken by that alertness, the dying away from the hold of the higher dream. The weak spirit quickens, but the life that stirs in it is the life of rebellion-death. The lost lilac, the lost sea voices, and the lost sea smell compound the subversion, with the repetitions both inciting and reflecting the nature of the lost heart, pulling it away into the now dominant meaning of the epithet. The bent golden rod points significantly downward.[21] The spirit is lost in refusing to be lost, in re-attaching itself to what it has relinquished. The betraying strength gathers with the repetition of 'quickens' and the unfamiliar energy, so far withheld from the natural world of the poem, in 'The cry of quail and the whirling plover.' The lures are starkly simple, yet overwhelming to the destitute mind. The deeply moving effect of the passage rests on the consciousness, everywhere apparent in the language, of the destructive force of the pull away from Eden, side by side with the recognition, also everywhere present in the language, that the pull for all its destructiveness remains inalienably an act of life. The blind eye creates, notwithstanding its blindness, and even though it can create no more than empty forms between the gates of illusion. Smell renews the salt savour of the sandy earth and the barrenness of what is gained is overcome by the caressing hunger of the sibilants.

The next stanza widens the distance of alienation and the protagonist who looked through the window at the granite shore can now be thought of as among the rocks which he longingly contemplated. Three dreams cross in a place of tension and twilight: the lower dream between the ivory gates, the dream of the higher reality, and most poignant of all, the dream that the mind can be securely taken over by the source of meaning it has all too briefly glimpsed. The blue of the rocks has acquired many associations from the poem's history: the blue of distraction, the blue of Mary's colour, and the blue of that ultimate interior where final choices are affirmed or denied. It is now also the blue of a separating distance, of the sea on which the voyager must embark. As the poem wheels back to its beginning, 'Teach us to care and not to care' takes on additional connotations. The right caring and the right indifference, precariously achieved in the struggle of the poem, must be renewed against the centripetal pull of the lower reality. Stillness must be found again and must be maintained as stillness against the removing force. So the line from the *Paradiso* is cited to remind us that the centre of peace is constant, whether we stand in wonder before the multifoliate rose, or walk in solitude among the blue rocks of exile. The second yew is shaken so that we can contrast the thousand whispers of the divided mind with the single statement of the true relationship that remains before us in the eternal or the turning world. The sister who is now also the mother is not only the spirit of the fountain and the garden, of the ordered forces of design and renewal, but is also the spirit of the river and the sea, of the destructive element which is within us and about us. The lines look forward unmistakably to a later poem which has not only yet to be written, but which will not, for several years, appear even on the horizon of the author's mind. In that poem the river and the sea will work their assault upon the world of meaning and the Lady's shrine will stand on a promontory, the farthest possible extension of those blue rocks.

The last lines of *Ash-Wednesday* invoke an ancient prayer, the Anima Christi, and a ritual response used in more than one service.[22] But these are not the words of a communicant approaching the altar. They are rather the beseeching words of the lost heart drifting away into the distance of alienation. The force of removal has prevailed increasingly in the final paragraphs, first in the longing look towards the granite cliffs, then in the pull of the natural order which the mind can characterize but which the blood cannot resist, and thirdly in the implied transference from the protected world behind the window to the perilously open world of the blue rocks. The countering assurance put before us in the quotation from Dante, the double role of the sister-mother and the consolation of the second yew, is that the divine presence is with us in the world as well as the World or, as Milton puts it, 'in vallie and in plaine,' as well as above the cliffs of Eden.[23] It is an assurance which acts mainly as a prelude to exile, a lifeline to the soul about to be separated. Even the paragraphing functions so as to bring the distancing momentum to its climax. As the words 'Suffer me not to be separated' stand separated on the page from the ritual response that follows, the last line in its isolation seems to cry out from a receding loneliness, imploring that the gulf between itself and the centre not be widened beyond the point of retrieval.

A rereading of *Ash-Wednesday* shows that it is considerably more than an exercise in piety or a psychological narrative of the progress of the soul. As an exploration of how paradise is lost it gains much of its force and some of its weight of sadness from a previous and continuing effort to rediscover paradise – an effort which in *Ash-Wednesday* reaches both its hard-won climax and its betrayal. Eliot's poetry has been urged forward by the conviction that the garden exists even and perhaps particularly for those who practise their profession between the gates of ivory. If the Word is betrayed by its sapient sutlers, the poet remains to achieve the movement of language and of the mind inhabiting language, from dialect to speech, and finally back to the single word and its multifoliate unity. The mind finds its way forward by divesting itself of evasions and distractions, by 'trying the experiment of attempting to form' a civilised but non-religious mentality, by seeking the garden in its own archaeology through the maximum penetration by the forma-tive consciousness. When the experiment fails, the terms of life are known and are known more clearly as the terms of life rather than death. The poetry can then move into an investi-gation of the cost and the fear of those terms. The true death takes place, the land is ours in its originating nothingness, the stairway is mounted, and the threshold is gained. But the blind eye must create its empty forms as well as grope its way to its enlightening visions. If it is not human nature it is at least the imagining and the making nature which is torn on the horn between those seasons of our being, of which mid-winter spring is the fleeting crystallisation. Eliot's poetry acts out the desolation of exile, the terror of life, and the tran-quillity of renewal. But it does not merely put these rhythms before us: it also convinces us of their interpenetration. The spiral turns out of darkness into light and again out of light into darkness. Renewal does not exempt us from the continu-ing ascent of the spiral.

CHAPTER FIVE

The Approach to the Meaning

Eliot wrote little poetry in the three years after *Ash-Wednesday*. The *Five-Finger Exercises* were published in *The Criterion* of January 1933 and *Triumphal March* made its initial appearance in 1931 as No. 35 of the *Ariel Poems*. The only other poem to be published during this period was *Difficulties of a Statesman* in *The Hound and Horn* of Autumn 1932 and in *Commerce* of Winter 1932. No attempt will be made to place the *Five-Finger Exercises* in relation to the Eliot continuity, but the two Coriolan poems, though lying to one side of the main line of movement, lie sufficiently close to it to reflect something of the nature of the movement.

It can be said, at least initially, that both poems are concerned with the substitute the world seeks for the Word. The true triumphal march is Christ's entry into Jerusalem. The false march calls for a surrogate less ornate and with a more varied freight of implication than jewelled unicorns drawing the gilded hearse. In 'manipulating a continuous parallel between antiquity and contemporaneity'[1] Rome provides a model of distraction for Europe and the boots of storm-troopers can be heard on an ancient pavement. Hitler had yet to come to power but, to the reader looking back, the gathering storm seems reflected in the martial music of the first line, the catalogue of weaponry taken nearly verbatim from Ludendorff's *The Coming War in Europe*[2] and, more significantly, in the crowd's attitude to leadership. The military contribution is succeeded by the civilian, as society and leisure affirm themselves in the golf club captains, the scouts, the gymnastic society, the liverymen, and the Mayor. The hero brings up the procession 'watchful, waiting, perceiving, indifferent'[3] in a pose which can convey judiciously poised detachment or masterful inattention to the real needs of his followers. The need for the Word which the substituted word satisfies is made clear by the symbol of the dove, by the running water of the freshened springs from the garden of *Ash-Wednesday*,. and by a line which, repeated in *Burnt Norton*, will become the centre of the final insight.

The sacrifice is made and the virgins emerge from the temple. The dust in their urns, the repetition of 'dust' and the pulverisation into 'Dust of dust' expound the empty splendour of the first line, now repeated. The relationship with the twice-repeated 'light' in the final paragraph is evident. We can make the point that man's mortality should drive us to some more lasting illumination than the brief flare of a match kindling a cigarette. For that matter a bell ringing on Easter day should remind us of the ground swell that is and was from the beginning and not of the possibility that crumpets are being served. However, if there is a relationship between man's mortality and the eternal light there is also a relationship between bread and circuses. Popular leaders, particularly in depression years, must learn to be superior sausage sellers.[4]

Early in the poem we encounter Husserl's observation that the natural wakeful life of the ego is a perceiving.[5] It is difficult to think of the voluble narrator as having read Husserl or for that matter, Charles Maurras, but Eliot has mixed voices before to suggest the overall misunderstanding. Here, the deflationary line which follows ('we can wait with our stools and sausages') shows the higher possibility drowned in the lower gabble. In returning to Husserl as we should, we find him asking how the constantly perceiving consciousness is to be separated from what it perceives. Eliot on the other hand is merely pointing out how far civilization and its resounding inanities push us back from the conditions of a normal waking life. In the most rudimentary sense the observers can see very little because of the crowd obscuring their view and because of the cordon formed by the soldiers round the hero. But the little they see is unfortunately sufficient to serve them as an embodiment of their 'higher' aspirations. They do not look behind the simulation to the potential emptiness, still less beyond it to the 'hidden' reality to which the true symbol should direct us, the true calm and the true detachment, the certainty which leaves 'no interrogation' in the eyes. As for the hero, he is described as 'perceiving' but what he perceives may be no more than the main chance, or the joint opportunity to serve both ego and state.

The false procession, the false lights, the bell falsely interpreted, and the mystique of the leader as a deliverance from the everyday are bound together in the final quotation. The listener in Charles Maurras's *L'Avenir de l'intelligence* is expressing incredulity that a procession should honour a man of letters and that soldiers should form a cordon round him.[6] But a writer is at least committed to the search for the hidden source and the true illumination. The real incongruity is that we should honour those who, instead of arousing the self to wakefulness, interpose themselves between the mind and its natural pursuit of reality.

Eliot took *Triumphal March* out of the Ariel series because he meant it 'to be the first of a sequence in the life of the character who appears in this first part as young Cyril.'[7] The second poem in this unfinished sequence is *Difficulties of a Statesman*. It is generally assumed that the protagonist of this poem is the hero of *Triumphal March* grown older, the parallel growth of Cyril being measured by his progress from crumpet consumer to telephone operator. But the hero and the statesman are complementary types and there is some point in treating the second poem as not simply the tale of Coriolanus subdued, or Coriolanus as he might have been had he been given his consulship. The leader governs by standing above accountability. The statesman governs by making himself accountable to the populace. Both ways are evasions of the true accountability. As the statesman seeks his mandate in the first lines of the poem, the real nature of that mandate is made evident. All flesh is grass and the just city can only be built if we build it in the image of the eternal city. This is the right cry but it does not win elections or lead to the crier being garlanded with oak leaves. So the committees proceed to work out the lower mandate and the rise of Cyril is measured not by the steps on the purgatorial stairway, but by the progressive steps of his salary increments with a Christmas bonus as the final flourish of parody. As the committees compound confusion instead of producing a consensus, the populace of frogs croaks mindlessly in the marshes,[8] the guards cast dice evoking the crucifixion, and the fireflies flare against the now faint lightning of that transforming event. The next cry is appropriately a cry for help but it does not follow the direction of the last line of *Ash-Wednesday*. After the wrong mandate has been accepted. it is the wrong mother who is supplicated and this rampant upholder of the Roman specification seems not to be endowed with Volumnia's understanding as she confronts her whimpering Coriolanus. He is a Hollow Man even in the mutilated manner in which he quotes those phrases of *Triumphal March* which adumbrated the presence of the eternal. His plea is not for the courage to advance into significance or even for Coriolanus's rage of self-sufficiency, that obstinate standing upon the ground of the ego which, though suicidal, was at least resolute. This statesman seeks instead a retreat into the womb, or a Kafkaesque regression into insect life. The twice-repeated 'RESIGN' of the final line, playing against the twice-repeated 'light' and the twice-repeated 'dust' of *Triumphal March* is cruelly appropriate. There is a resignation leading to the discovery that our peace is in His will. There is also that resignation from true responsibility with which the promises of a statesman begin.

The satire in the *Coriolan* poems can be telling but it should also be evident that Eliot's dismissal of leaders who led nowhere and servants who served only the hydra-headed monster of the populace was not in the main current of the times. The house of Faber itself, with Eliot as one of its directors, was publishing poetry led by a different vision. Both Eliot and Auden might have agreed that it was time for the destruction of error and that the chairs needed to be brought in from the land of lobelias and tennis flannels. But there was another world of long lines of the unemployed, of water-filled mine shafts and deserted shipyards, an ice age of dereliction for which Auden found the poetry. For Spender religion was 'the church blocking the sun.' 'Man shall be man'[9] he proclaimed in an ardent tautology, reflecting Shelley's view of the human fraternity after the unbinding of Prometheus. Another poet asked those who loved England and 'had an ear for her music' to listen and hear 'the entrance of a new tune.'[10] Eliot was busy restoring an 'ancient rhyme.' The stranger in *The Rock* laments that 'every son would have his motor cycle,/And daughters ride away on casual pillions.'[11] A thirties poet on the other hand invokes the weekend swarms who 'go out in tandem or on pillions' as those who would find 'long-lost kinship and restore the blood's fulfillment.'[12] It is the Marxist brotherhood, not the Christian community, which constitutes fulfillment, though the brotherhood is merged in that organic society which has been an enduring dream of English poetry.

In Eliot's work we see the unfolding and the forming of a mind in its wakeful occupation of perceiving and pursuing the meaningful, as beauty (which can be thought of as the design of meaning) is traditionally pursued in the calling of the poet. *Ash-Wednesday* occupies its proper place in that unfolding, consummating a previous momentum and opening out into the solitude among the rocks that must follow. But *Ash-Wednesday* is the work of the man and not the moment, unless we are thinking of those timeless moments of which history as we finally know it is the pattern. *The Waste Land* and *The Hollow Men* spoke *for* as well as *to* a generation. Eliot's later poetry speaks to its time and to others; but it can only do so at the cost of withdrawal from the time which it addresses.

By the middle thirties it could have been thought that Eliot's career was drawing to an honourable close. The *Coriolan* sequence lay unfinished. The choruses to *The Rock*, though they have been unduly deprecated, were concerned with declamation rather than exploration. The Page Barbour lectures delivered at the University of Virginia in 1933 seemed the work of a Christian rather than a literary polemicist. The Norton lectures delivered at Harvard showed us a critic becoming an institution. The earlier criticism had been specific yet representative in its often barbed pointings, exciting yet civilizing the taste of a generation. The later work was more guarded and in the end less instructive. With the publication of *Selected Essays* (1932) and *Collected Poems, 1909-1935* one could conclude that the writer was putting his accomplishment together. Yeats had done this when less than half of his literary life was over; but writing obituaries is easier for the critic than learning from the past. The obituary writer could see the poetry after *Ash-Wednesday* trailing off into what were helpfully arranged as Unfinished Poems, Minor Poems, and choruses from a joint work. At the end of this regulated exit was a poem called *Burnt Norton*.

Before beginning *Murder in the Cathedral* in 1934, Eliot had visited friends in Chipping Camden. Outside the Gloucestershire town was a house called Burnt Norton, so named because of a fire set by its owner, Sir William Keyte, in October 1741. It is now a private school for maladjusted boys.[13] It would be fitting to think that as Eliot wandered through the grounds and formal garden of this house, there came into his mind the meditation which was to become the beginning of the most unusual long poem in the English language. The deflationary truth is that no potential poem came into Eliot's mind and that the poem which eventually shaped itself round the occasion was a by-product of his dramatic interests. Lines and fragments had been discarded from *Murder in the Cathedral* because the producer did not think they would go over on the stage and because Eliot 'humbly bowed to his judgement.' Gradually a poem formed around these lines and fragments. 'In the end it came out as *Burnt Norton*.' Up to this point Eliot had thought that 'pure unapplied poetry was in the past' for himself, and even after this point his increasing absorption in writing for the stage might have left *Burnt Norton* to stand alone. But the war threw him back on himself.

East Coker was the result and it was 'only in writing *East Coker*' that Eliot 'began to see the Quartets as a set of four.'[14] Accident can scarcely have played a greater part in a poem universally admired for its design. If, as Hugh Kenner argues, the form of *The Waste Land* was the product of Pound's scissors,[15] we can allow ourselves amazement as well as gratitude, first for the unplanned retrieval of that fortuitous form and then for its incorporation into a macro-form, with four progressive deployments of the same structure fitted into a structure that both re-enacted and summed them. The extraordinary poetic accomplishment of *Burnt Norton* was noted when the poem appeared. in an important review in *Scrutiny*.[16] But the seminal nature of the accomplishment only becomes apparent when possession of the completed symbol enables us to know the place for the first time.

Dame Helen Gardner sees each of the Quartets as a five-movement structure in which the first movement 'consists of statement and counter-statement in a free blank verse.' It is 'built on contradictions which the poem is to reconcile.' The second movement 'opens with a highly "poetical" lyric passage' followed by 'an extremely colloquial passage, in which the idea which had been treated in metaphor and symbol in the first half of the movement is expanded, and given personal application.' The third movement 'is the core of each poem out of which reconciliation grows: it is an exploration, with a twist, of the ideas of the first two movements.' The fourth movement is a lyric and the fifth is again in two parts, recapitulating 'the themes of the poem with personal and topical applications' and 'making a resolution of the discords' of the first movement.[17] Dame Helen is properly sensitive to the wide range of variations which is played against this structure and the dangers of proceeding to the individual poems with too rigid an expectation of how they are to behave. Her account remains the classic statement of the form of the Quartets, supplemented by C.K. Stead's examination of cross-connections between the four poems – an examination that is more than successful in showing the severe standards of formal relatedness which the Quartets are capable of surviving.[18] Hugh Kenner's characteristically responsive analysis, which is carried further by Denis Donoghue, basically accepts Dame Helen's view of the five-part dialectic in each of the Quartets as well as the derivation of that dialectic from *The Waste Land*.[19] Within this frame he sees the 'central structural principle' displayed in the central section of *Burnt Norton* as 'opposites falsely reconciled, then truly reconciled.'[20]

When the recurrent form of the Quartets has been perceived it becomes desirable to acknowledge their diversity and to investigate the question of how they add to each other in repeating each other. Four element groupings which join in an accepted totality are a natural way of outlining this connectedness. Thus we can have the Quartets identified respectively with air, earth, water, and fire (Stead); with early summer, late summer, autumn, and winter (Kenner); with grace, faith, hope, and charity (Kirk); and in the fourth sections with the Unmoved mover, the redeeming Son, the Virgin, and the Holy Ghost (Kenner).[21] Perhaps a more profitable procedure is to take a 'subject' common to the poems and, by examining its various orchestrations, to seek to ascertain the nature of the movement through the poems and the place of each poem in relation to that movement. Time in *Burnt Norton*, for instance, is abstract and impersonal, time told by the philosopher's clock. Time in *East Coker* is familial and hierarchic, the pendulum swinging to the rhythms of Ecclesiastes and to the growth and subsidence of the individual life. Time in *The Dry Salvages* is elemental, older than the time of chronometers, rung by the ground swell that was 'from the beginning.' Time in *Little Gidding* is time humanised as history, measured not in duration but significance, able to form 'a pattern of timeless moments.' If we now take up the other subject, 'pattern,' to which time is linked in the last quotation, we find in *Burnt Norton* that 'the detail of the pattern is movement' but also that it is only by the pattern that words or music can 'reach the stillness.' Both understandings are a comment on *Four Quartets* and the contrary propulsions on which the poems are built: immersion in the flux and the passion to escape from it. The way up and the way down are the same. *East Coker* takes up the subject with a more urgent sense of the perils of immersion, an anguished perception of Heraclitus's maxim that we cannot step twice into the same river. Knowledge 'derived from experience' is knowledge of the past, irrelevant because it is past. It imposes a pattern on the present, falsifying the present because 'the pattern is new in every moment.' Life does not broaden from precedent to precedent, the accumulation ordered by the wisdom of the years. As we grow older 'the world becomes stranger, the pattern more complicated.' In *The Dry Salvages* the extreme of immersion is reached, the redeeming recognitions declare themselves on the brink and the mind is informed by the sense of 'another pattern.' The otherness is crucial in its suggestion of recourse to a different dimension and in amending the consciousness in *East Coker* of the relativity of pattern, formed and re-formed in the flux, as well as the consciousness earlier in *The Dry Salvages*, that there may be no pattern at all but only reiteration. Finally *Little Gidding* takes up and transmutes the language of both *East Coker* and *The Dry Salvages* as history becomes 'a pattern of timeless moments' and as 'faces and places' vanish 'to become renewed, transfigured in another pattern.'[22]

As we study these varying orchestrations, each so meticulously adjusted to the precise stage reached in the forward and circling movement, we become more sharply aware of the kind of poem we are being invited to enter. The deception of the thrush is not the song of the sirens; but it is a warning that poetry can be deceptive, though capable of being the way to that knowledge that is only possible when we advance through our illusions. The poem can define these illusions adequately because its alternations of the lyric and discursive make it an act of self-consciousness recurrently reviewing the advancing consciousness. It is structurally shaped to require its own interpretation. It is not merely natural but inevitable that an act of language so devised should periodically review the nature of language. This is the basis for the recurrent remarks on language in the fifth section. The impending reconciliation which is to form the climax of the poem is preceded by the reminder that a concern with significance is a concern with speech. If there is a resolution, words find it, or betray it.

Yeats came into his strength and words obeyed his call. Later he beat on the wall and truth answered the imperious summons. To Eliot language is not the resisting-consenting mistress, or the rebellious steed whom one can rejoice in subduing. The complete consort can dance together but only when the commerce of words celebrates the commerce of thought. Much struggling is necessary to find that easy relationship in which language and meaning recognize their destiny in each other.

The poet in *Burnt Norton* is dignified but not wholly invisible.[23] The 'perhaps' of the second line introduces the Oxbridge voice. We are aware of the intent, philosophical intelligence using language as a speculative instrument. 'Words after speech, reach/Into the silence' and one is persuaded that they do so by the force of extension in them, by the rhyme stretching the open vowel, while the end of the line keeps it from its objective. It remains connected to that objective by the penetrative weight of 'Into' beginning the next line. We must be responsive also to the possibilities stirred by 'Words after speech.' When speech ends silence begins, but there is also an end to the structures of thought that are articulated in language. To render silence in words, to render stillness in motion, is possible only by achieving the stasis of pattern, a condition prior to becoming, as in a Chinese jar, or as in Keats's Grecian Urn, that 'still unravished bride of quietness.' Yet the jar still 'Moves perpetually in its stillness' and once again the language persuades us by living out the proposition, by its agitation of stillness, by its sense of the work of art as the mimesis of the unmoved mover. Then we move on to stillness reached not by stasis but by infinite prolongation, the lingering note of the violin, stillness not contemplated but performed. The true stillness is not that, though that may be a way of approaching it. Words and music move 'only in time' and there is wit enough here to remind us that the poet is something more than the dogged explorer. But what moves in time must co-exist with and reflect what is beyond time. If not, it is 'only living' and can 'only die.' We pass through a series of attempts to define the relationship of the end and the beginning, the strain increasing with the effort of definition and ending with the emphatic 'all is always now.' We can discriminate the phrase from 'all time is eternally present' which preceded it in the poem and 'Quick, now, here, now, always –' which is to follow. The range of vivifications – poised statement, strenuous reaching, and excited discovery – indicate some of the approximations which surround the idea and gather together our knowledge of its stillness; but they also indicate how the idea inhabits a world and how it can begin to be not merely cognized but lived with. The stretching of language into the centre is difficult but it is also for one type of mind (which is Eliot's), the beckoning margin of the poetic enterprise. 'All is always now' by its strenuousness leads naturally into an inventory of these difficulties, piling up formidably to suggest a mountain quite other than the hill of truth. But the obstacles which the mind vehemently lists in the immediacies of frustration are, as we might expect, set down with a purpose. Words strain, crack, and break because worn by usage, they can no longer carry the weight of meaning. They slip, slide, and perish in their endeavour to inch forward to the summit. They decay with imprecision, in a forewarning of the erosions of time which the subsequent Quartets are remorselessly to explore. They will not stay in place in their rebellion against that decorum, the passing of which *East Coker* is to lament and the restoration of which *Little Gidding* is to celebrate. They will not stay still: since this is a poem with several images of childhood we can think of the poet-schoolmaster scolding refractory children. The irony is that the mind not only cannot stay still but must use its disturbing energies to the maximum in order to close in on the stillness. The suppressed image of scolding carries into the next sentence where the effort to compose the music that touches reality is continuously assailed by the noises and voices of illusion, 'scolding, mocking, or merely chattering.' The frustration of the effort has been fully worked through and it can now be added that the frustration may be mimetic. The Word in solitude, at the centre of silence, is also attacked by voices of unreality. The attempt to reach stillness through motion, the heart of the undertaking in this particular Quartet, fails in its nature and yet may succeed in its failure.

The waste of war hangs over *East Coker*, the failure of the civilizing effort, the questions flung by catastrophe at the endeavour of intelligence. It is necessary to begin again, to face the obsolescence of what one took to be pertinence. The pattern is new in every moment and the poem will never cease to be rewritten. 'One has only learnt to get the better of words/ For the thing one no longer has to say, or the way in which/ One is no longer disposed to say it.' This is a comment in the first place on the breakdown of continuity, on the irrelevance of the past as it faces the present in its destructive uniqueness. It is also a comment on Eliot's own unremitting effort to get the better of words, with each step on the stairway making the next step possible and yet demanding a wholly new act of language in which the next step can be negotiated. In this poem published in the year of Dunkirk, with the German army poised across the Channel, the attitude to language resembles that of an exasperated sergeant towards an ill-trained and badly-equipped body of home guards. Words and music once reached into the silence. Undisciplined squads of emotion now take part in a commando raid on the inarticulate. The inarticulate is a poor substitute for the word unable to speak a word and what the raids presumably bring back is not intelligence of the infinite but a slightly more adequate knowledge of ourselves. These diminished objectives fit a situation in which we must begin at the beginning and in which the entire curve of the poet's œuvre, searchingly achieved in successive acts of language, is to be submitted again to the brutality of experience and discovered once more in the face of its assault. 'There is only the fight to recover what has been lost/And found and lost again and again.'[24] The bleakness of the phrase is all the more telling because the poet has found and lost the garden in *Ash-Wednesday* and found it again in the enclosed world of *Burnt Norton*.

The Dry Salvages has no discussion of language, not because of the author's absent-mindedness, or his failure to conform to the critic's view of his structures, but because the fifth section deals with what we can know of the Word. The point of intersection of time and the timeless should be the climax of any raid, not on the inarticulate but on the inaccessible. It is the point where the silence can be touched, where the mind makes itself tangential to the stillness. Speech finds not only its beginning but its sustaining dimension when the impossible union of spheres of existence is actual. It accepts that discovery without comment and one hopes therefore without qualification. In the poem that is to follow, the discovery can irradiate the world which it makes significant.

In *Little Gidding* the main remarks on language are in parenthesis as if to suggest to us that when all words are at home they become incidental to the understandings to which they direct us. At the same time the 'complete consort' dancing together links itself to another kind of parenthesis in *East Coker* when dancing signified the commodious sacrament and concord of matrimony, in a quotation from Elyot's *The Governor*. That quotation was made in the original spelling as if to imply the obsolescence of tradition and the archaic nature of concord in a world laid open to the destructive fire of war. In *Little Gidding* the conception does not strain against its context and in celebrating the marriages of language, the poem has also advanced to a restoration of more basic relationships, an easy commerce of the old and new. There is commerce too across the segregations of diction with the common word 'exact without vulgarity' and the formal word 'precise but not pedantic' joining each other in the inclusive statement. 'My dame sing for this person accurate songs' is Wallace Stevens's request to the lady of poetry[25] and Eliot's commitment throughout his work has been to accurate song rather than careless rapture, to re-establishing that language environment where 'passion and precision have been one.'[26] The poem's taking up of its past at this point also goes back to the encircling motto phrases of *East Coker* in its remarks that the end is where we start from and that to make an end is to make a beginning. Much further back lie the posings of a lady for her portrait: 'But our beginnings never know our ends.' *East Coker* takes up that recognition with dejection and dignity. Broken expectations call for a wholly new start and a different kind of failure. The persistence in the civilizing effort to which every writer is party implies that an end, a decisive frustration, is to be thought of as calling for a new beginning; but the understanding is faced with fortitude rather than lived into language. In *Little Gidding* the timbre of the rephrasing registers once more the advance that has been made on the stairway. Finally *Burnt Norton* is remembered and the words that would not stay in place now take their places 'to support each other.' The language which decayed with imprecision in the first quartet and deteriorated 'into the general mess of imprecision of feeling' in the second, is now blessed with exactness and stability. Yet every completed act of language is an epitaph, 'a symbol perfected in death.' It is an end that can invite a new beginning not because it fails but rather because it succeeds.

Further indications can be given of the way in which recurrent subjects are taken up in the recurrent forms and of how the orchestration and nuancing help to define both the spiralling flow of the movement through the recurrences and the manner in which each form opens itself to the movement and urges it forward. Enough evidence has been provided to make the point and the point is not simply that we should respond with appreciation to the poem's cohesiveness of design, its planetary wheelings of intricacy. Appreciation is due but it is surely due also to the intellectual stamina, the sheer solidity of the cognitive effort that is able to evolve and to maintain so complete a relatedness through such a range of registers.

Studies of the Quartets tend either to concentrate on the recurrent form and the more important of the deployments made within it, or to accompany the poem in its course with some attention to aftersight and foresight. Yet as the poem itself suggests, the relationship of process to pattern is crucial to its character, if only because it provides the aesthetic mimesis of the relationship of motion to stillness and of time to eternity. To adapt a line already quoted, the pattern is new in every poem, yet with a constancy in its modelling of the actual that makes it both a way of containment and a means of exploration. The detail of the pattern is movement or to put it only slightly differently, what we see as a structure is transmitted as a movement. Form is authenticated by experience but experience must also be found capable of form, of revealing some of the penetrations of stillness, notwithstand-

ing its corrosions and betrayals. There is indeed no other possibility if our concern is to find the pivots of speech and to
maintain them as controlling entities in what could otherwise
be the unformed tide of language.

One of the issues raised as we consider, or move into, the
relationship of pattern to process, is the relationship of recurrent form to enclosing form. Professor Kenner is one of the
few critics who have given this matter any thought and his
suggestion teases us with the possibility that just as the individual poems are built around a statement and counter-statement with a parodic reconciliation followed by a true one, so
the entire series may be built around the opposition between
Burnt Norton and *East Coker*, with a delusive resolution in
The Dry Salvages followed by the true light of *Little Gidding.*[27] A correspondence can thus be established between
macro and micro forms but only at the cost of having *The
Dry Salvages* placed outside the pattern of recurrence. Its
false reconciliation would then be followed not by a true
one, but by one purporting to be true but even more deva-
statingly false. There is a wrong way of apprehending the Incarnation and *The Dry Salvages* exercises our vigilance by
putting that way before us. This view of the third quartet as
finally parodic results from the newly-found dislike of the
poem's language[28] and is part of the modern willingness to resort to the hypothesis of deliberate parody as a saving device.
The foreign hand, not to mention the nervous breakdown,
once had a similar function in disposing of literary embarrass-
ments. It is questionable whether *The Dry Salvages* needs to
be salvaged in this way but for the time being it will suffice
to note that there are other ways of linking macro and micro
forms which do not exact so startling a price.

In pondering the relationship of recurrent form to enclosing form, we should remain aware of the enclosing form's
relationship to the œuvre which it inherits and moves forward. If we say that *Four Quartets* brings into poetic life the
rhythms of exile and renewal, we must remember how the
previous poetry has made us respond to the dominance of
these rhythms and how the closing turn in *Ash-Wednesday* in
particular has been the turn out of renewal into exile. *Burnt*

Norton can begin classically in the garden only because the garden has been found to exist, though mainly by the presence of its absence as a lost dimension of the civilized consciousness. The nature of that consciousness is to resist the imputation of its insufficiency, the suggestion that it is not capable on its own grounds of knowing its own roots. The early poetry takes on itself the protracted and difficult task of proclaiming that insufficiency, not against but through the resisting consciousness. It is able to attain or rather uncover its objective through the cross-play of irony and involvement, a cross-play which allows us both to stand within and to stand apart from the mind's frustration of itself in the impasses of its own evasions. The investigative, eventually débris-searching effort advances the consciousness to a brink at which another dimension can manifest itself, but only at the pillars of the known world. The awareness of exile, the hearing of the terms of renewal, make it possible for a stairway to be mounted, a threshold to be gained, a mountain range crossed into another country, and new ships to be discerned upon a changed horizon. We can begin again in the garden, look over the wall as Buddha did, confront the potentially crippling question, and find no alternative to the long road to enlightenment. The myth of loss and recovery moves into the understanding that the meaning is in the recovery, that the enclosed garden is a refuge rather than a shaping principle, until it is laid open to the assault of time and the world. The way forward is the way back, not simply in the sense of Heraclitus's maxim, or in the additional sense of Vaughan's *The Retreate*, but in a sense more distinctive to the American vision, the conviction that the frontier is the source.

If in mythic terms the Quartets enact the loss and the recovery of Eden, they are, in terms of the poem of the mind, a movement from concept through experience to meaning. In personal terms they are the life journey from a first world to what as nearly as possible is a final one, from the individual to the traditional and historic. In ancestral terms they reenact a migration and celebrate a return. Four related depths of movement should be sufficient for four quartets, but it needs to be added that as in any poem of enduring dimensions, the creative force of this particular cycle is called out by a contemporary challenge. It is the war which renders un-inhabitable what might otherwise be a protected garden, which makes it impossible to grow old gently, which demands exposure as the price of renewal. Those 'twenty years largely wasted, the years of *l'entre deux guerres*' launch the poem into 'the dark cold and the empty desolation.' And it is in an unreal city lit by the ravaging flames of war that the poem draws together its crowned knot of understanding. The act of meaning that a work of art seeks to accomplish becomes more potent when it is sustained against the resistance of some great mockery, that goes beyond personal circumstance and seems sufficiently wide to question the nature of life. It is in confronting and resolutely responding to this question within a formal sophistication which the question cannot de-stroy and to which it is eventually made to contribute, that *Four Quartets* achieves its status as a work for our times.

<h2 style="text-align:center">II</h2>

We begin not in the garden, but in what we can think of as a study that overlooks it. The introductory voice is quiet, poised, its tonality characterised by the donnish 'perhaps.' Eliot's favourite tactic of interwoven repetitions that unfold and reconsider an evolving relationship is with us from the outset. The significant departure from the intertwining of time and presence is the word 'contained' which plants in the opening, the encircling possibilities of *East Coker*, the begin-ning considered as seed and the end considered as core. 'All time is irredeemable' the fifth line affirms, if we agree that all time is eternally present. The line places itself in relationship with *Ash-Wednesday*'s call to redeem the time and *Little Gid-ding*'s conclusion that a people can be redeemed from time only by possession of its history. The eternally present, the completely patterned, is above redemption. The incomplete in time's element seeks redemption. For the moment, the finality of the statement governs the footfalls in the memory, the irretrievability of the 'might have been.' 'My words echo/ Thus, in your mind' the voice says, calling to the answering experience in ourselves, and we are once more drawn into the journey as Prufrock involved us in the first line of the œuvre. Even Prufrock's 'Do not ask what is it' is echoed as the speaker declines to specify a purpose so tentative at this stage that it merely disturbs the dust on a bowl of rose leaves.

The irretrievability of the 'might have been' gives urgency to the 'now,' the impulsive, ironically irretrievable movement, through the first gate and into the first world. It is a world of unreal reality where the guests are 'invisible,' the music 'unheard,' and the eyebeams (an odd revival of pre-Renaissance optics)[29] 'unseen.' But the guests are 'dignified,' they accept and are accepted in a decorum which the subsequent poems are to question, and they move in a formal pattern, anticipating the patterns of movement in the lyric which is to follow. If this is a child's world of concealment and discovery,[30] it is also an initiation into a poet's world where the real is found to be so by the declarative force of the imagination. Later when 'There they were' extends itself into the strenuous 'there' of the still point, it will also become the world of the passionate metaphysician.

In *The Dry Salvages* a shaft of sunlight dissipates the distractions on the stairway of *Ash-Wednesday* and music is unheard because it is heard so deeply that it is not music at all. The pool in the formal garden of *Burnt Norton* is not only dry but brown-edged from continued dryness. Yet it is filled with water out of sunlight in a sudden efflorescence of two forces of renewal and the lotus rises out of the heart of the abundance, 'quietly, quietly,' in the breathlessness of timelessness.[31] A cloud passes, the pool is empty, and we are taken back to the image of that wide and empty sea which follows the encounter with the hyacinth girl in *The Waste Land*. Yet the deception of the thrush is also a protection for a humankind which 'cannot bear very much reality' and which is sheltered by the 'weakness of the changing body' from the demanding purity of heaven. The illuminated and necessarily fugitive moment, the plenitude succeeded by the emptiness, suffices within the terms of time to indicate the 'one end which is always present.' The 'might have been' would not have manifested that end any more fully than the 'what has been.' Even God, according to Aquinas, cannot undo the past, though this is no problem to the advocates of doublethink, but if the past were otherwise it would continue to affirm a constant pattern, the difference lying only in the language of events.[32]

Mallarmé is said to be the inspiration behind the first line of section II.[33] If so we must concede a considerable imaginative distance between thunder and rubies and sapphire and garlic. The axletree could have come from Chapman, from Milton's *Ode on the Nativity*, from *Burbank with a Baedeker*, or from a variety of other places. Garlic and sapphires are seen by Chiari as representing 'the temporal and perennial elements of life,' by Grover Smith as representing gluttony and avarice, and by Harry Blamires as symbolizing 'the paradoxically combined crudity and charm, earthiness and sparkle, of the human flesh in which the tree of life is temporally grounded.'[34] As for the axletree, we can content ourselves with Kenner's view that it 'appears to be that of the turning heavens, its lower end, like the bole of Yggdrasill embedded in our soil.'[35] We might note that the turning movement, our main approach to the apprehension of the still point, is 'clotted' by what the world holds to be valuable as well as by what it considers vulgar. We should then try to see the image in balance with the one that succeeds it. The 'trilling wire' does sing below inveterate scars. In our response to reality there is an answering as well as an obstructive element. At this stage in the poem's rejoinder to itself these contrary impulsions can still be held within the frame of two great Elizabethan commonplaces – the world as dance and the world as macrocosm. The dance along the artery and the circulation of the lymph are figured in the drift of stars and one has to note with appreciation the slowing down through 'dance,' 'circulation,' and 'drift' to what could become by extension the stasis of eternity. We ascend the tree to a summer which may well be the prognosis of the 'unimaginable zero summer' of *Little Gidding*. Looking down on the leaves which were 'full of children' in a previous moment of excited disclosure, we can see their figuration affirming the pattern of things. Below, the boarhound and the boar continue the strife which is also part of the pattern. Contraries are reconciled in the higher distance. Both the clotting and the singing have their places and the lotus grows out of the mud of garlic and sapphires.

In the inner quartets the second part of the second movement is a colloquial taking up of the previous lyric. In the outer quartets, the taking up is more formal as if to suggest a regularity that is initially lost and finally recovered. The encounter scene in *Little Gidding* is in a metrically strict form seeking to recreate the equivalent of *terza rima* in English. The disquisition on the still point in *Burnt Norton* is in language of remarkable tautness and intentness, a maximum awareness of design expressed with a maximum effort at lucidity. The neither-nor technique can become metaphysical droning with lesser voices including the voice of Eliot himself when his sense of the stillness is less than fully extended. Here it operates to deprive the mind of any possible orientation, any point at which it can place itself in relation to the still point. At the same time the negative accumulation builds up a substantiality more weighty than the sum of the prepossessions it displaces. Not every litany of denials can accomplish this result. It is necessary to take account of the mind's customary lodgements, to refuse to let it come to rest, to have it taken over, not despite but because of its effort of intelligence. 'Neither flesh nor fleshless' could so easily be 'neither flesh nor spirit' but the movement to the alternative has been anticipated. Discontinuity is ruled out, yet continuity cannot be admitted. 'Neither from nor towards' dismisses our sense of the point as origin and the point as objective. Yet in a sense to be enacted by the circle of the four poems, the point can be apprehended as both origin and objective. 'Neither arrest nor fixity' rules out the possibility that the point can be known when motion ceases, when time stops, or when location (which implies space) is unambiguous and unalterable. 'Neither ascent nor decline' disposes of the ontological possibility of upward movement into the ultimate unity, or of decline (the reader's mind is presumed to be vigilant enough to have already discarded 'descent') into an atomistic diversity in which the still point might be known as an ultimate otherness. When terminology seeks to imply that which is beyond terminology, 'there is only the dance' as the defining effort itself insists, the movement from position to position in the circulation of understanding, the progressive surrounding by designed exclusions of what must finally be left to declare itself. That the point *is* is confirmed not only by what it is not, but by the finality of seizure in the verse, the three consecutive, anchoring stresses of 'at the still point there the dance is' cognising it decisively as Pound's unwobbling pivot.

If we can only say 'there we have been,' the meaning of the 'there' is in the residue of our response to its presence. The paragraph which follows is a delimitation not of what or where the point is, but of how it is experienced. Release from desire and the wheel of action and suffering, from the circle of the exterior and the interior tyranny, nevertheless leaves us 'surrounded' by a creative encirclement which both contains and frees us. The effort to define is important here if all is not to be lost in the fatal blur of the illuminated moment. 'A grace of sense' captures the encirclement in its latent paradox, elaborating 'neither flesh nor fleshless' while the 'white light still and moving' is the 'heart of light,' now circumference rather than centre, tranquil but also moving and vibrant with life. Then follows the word 'Erhebung,' daringly imported into the ardent context, another language raided for exactness, a reminder that while apprehension may be passionate, it is to be 'passionate only through a powerful and regulated intellect.'[36] Concentration without elimination is the heart of translucency. The still point is not the vanishing point. It remains a point where the partial ecstacy is completed and the partial horror (remembering *The Family Reunion*) is resolved. 'All manner of thing shall be well' but they are made well in different ways which it is the work of an active language to discriminate. Yet the consummation is not to be unreservedly sought. The 'enchainment of past and future/Woven in the weakness of the changing body' is a protection as well as an ensnarement. The strength of 'enchainment,' increased by its reflection in 'changing,' the way in which the alliteration doubles the involvement of 'woven' with 'weakness' are significant in suggesting that the extent of protection may even depend on the degree of entanglement. That 'flesh cannot endure' heaven and damnation brings the recoil from the still point to its climax and one is entitled to wonder whether the unremitting sight of heaven is not felt as damnation by the less-than-regenerate heart. The strain of continuing vision is well documented and can begin with Adam 'Dazzl'd and spent' after his 'Colloquy sublime' with God in the garden.[37] But we should also think of the point in the *Bhagavad Gita* when Arjuna at his own request is allowed to look into the crucible of the ultimate, the unbearable co-presence of creativeness and destructiveness, and begs to have restored to him the familiar figure of Krishna, his charioteer.[38]

The mind moving away from the still point is aware of its loss as well as of its safeguarding limitations. Time future and time past allow only a little consciousness and there are tones of deprivation in the word 'allow.' That to be conscious is not to be in time is a further and firmer statement of what is relinquished in the retreat from eternity. Nevertheless, the moment that is later to be characterised as 'in and out of time' can be remembered only in time and it is only by the incorporation of these moments into time that past and future, the enchainment of the mind but also its life-giving stream, can be placed in approximation to their final relationship. 'Only through time, time is conquered' is an adequate summary of this argument but 'conquered' is, quite deliberately, not a word which fits into the penumbra of a grace of sense. It is a word from the flux, from Heraclitean strife, issuing from time in asserting its victory over it.

Contrasted with the 'there' of the still point is a 'here,' a place of disaffection, inhabited not even by time past and time future, but by the barren succession of time before and time after. The descent into the underground for which the model is apparently Eliot's daily journey from Gloucestor Road to Russell Square Station[39] takes place in both *Burnt Norton* and *East Coker*. In the corresponding section of *The Dry Salvages* there is a journey by train and on 'the deck of the drumming liner.' In *Little Gidding* there is an implied journey to death. The descent is into a false darkness, death-in-life in those enormous daily migrations that keep the wheels which are not the true wheels turning. To attain the true darkness, which as *East Coker* tells us is the darkness of God, one must descend lower into the night of the soul. Meanwhile the wind sweeps the 'gloomy hills' of the unreal city (seven are appropriately and specifically listed), on none of which the true church is to be found.

The way up is the ascent to God 'through contemplation of created things.' The deepening cognisance of form is invested with a 'lucid stillness' which we can think of as a further reading of the grace of sense. Time does not come to a stop but its 'slow rotation' can be suggestive of permanence. A partial horror can be resolved and a shadow similarly turned into transient beauty. If the way up is that of enrichment, the way down is that of deprivation. The mind strips itself and silences itself, either by an intense effort to do so or by a withdrawal from all effort which brings about the same result by comprehensively negating the character of mind. These are the two ways down, to be contrasted with the way up, but as the second epigraph from Heraclitus has already advised us, the way up and the way down are the same. Between the two movements into reality lies the twittering world of distraction from distraction, that world which Eliot's earlier poetry has already filled with embodiments of emptiness. The Virgilian echoes here have been noted by critics[40] but the twittering also points to an unreality considerably less vital than the deception of the thrush. It is the difference between everyday and poetic illusion.

For Grover Smith the sunflower in section IV is associated with the Son and the clematis with the Virgin Mary. The kingfisher is a type of Christ. Headings observes that several critics see the kingfisher as the Fisher king and the yew as representing the Father. According to Blamires there is a probable reference to the Church in the image of the kingfisher's wing.[41] This determination to find and to systematize an interior reading can result in inadequate attention being paid to the poem's less indirect invitations. We should also be aware of the bell as anticipating the bell of *The Dry Salvages*, the cloud as remembering the cloud that passed over the sunlight-filled pool in section I, and the sunflower and clematis as fingerings of light, with a significant weakening from the turning of the sunflower to the straying down of the clematis. Spray and tendril in their delicacy partly subvert the force of 'clutch and cling,' making us aware of the fragile means and the imperative effort. In a poem so concerned with time the lyric is shaped appropriately as one side of an hourglass. The neck is in 'chill,' the narrow strait of our mortality. The yew's alliterative reachings have a finality which the same alliteration lacked in its earlier use. Then the light returns in the scintillation of the kingfisher's wing, the *li* repeatedly reflected and reversed as *il* in the answering mirror. The last reflection is in the word 'still,' invoking a word-play by which Eliot has already been charmed. The point is unmoving but it can also remain with us as endless duration in the movement of time.

Burnt Norton moves from an intimate disquisition, the voice talking across the study table, to a moment of illumination, the recollected quick of the here and now. The scope expands in the 'reconciling lyric' of section II, from the 'sodden floor' to the drifting stars in the heavens. In the remainder of section II, we move farther upwards to the ultimacy of the still point. In section III we move further downwards through the false and eventually into the true darkness, completing the circle in terms of the Heraclitean epigraph. The lyric of section IV balances the two extremities, the moment of the yew tree against the moment of the rose. Despite the slight, metaphysical shudder which those curling fingers of yew excite, it would be imperceptive to conclude that one moment stands for creativeness and the other for destructiveness. The double yews in *Animula* and *Ash-Wednesday* should already have educated us against such a reading. Both moments are essential in the significance of life and, as *Little Gidding* will later teach us, both moments are of 'equal duration.'

The final section of *Burnt Norton* takes up, as has already been noted, the relationship of language to the ultimate. It is a concern sanctioned both by the poem's structural requirement of self-scrutiny and by the first of the Heraclitean epigraphs. There is indeed. for those committed to the achievement of meaning in words, a distinctive connection between the two epigraphs. If the logos is common to all and each man yet lives as if he had a private wisdom of his own, the responsibility of the writer is to move from personal experience, through dialect evolving into speech, to the final understanding and the shaping stillness. In achieving this advance, he must progressively shape an integrity that will fully explore and preserve each level of relatedness and yet will keep each level in just proportion to the final dependence. He does so not by relinquishing language, by abandoning words in order to pass beyond words, but by using language with maximum intentness, to discover the presences by which words are irradiated. The way up and the way down are the same.

The final paragraph introduces a new relationship: that between love and desire. Less conceptual than the relationship between time and the timeless, or between stillness and motion, or between pattern and change, it nevertheless comprises these relationships and returns them to their locus in experience. The understandings worked out in the poem now move into a pattern of summation, negotiated through interlocking repetitions that spiral into place round a crucial mutation of the word 'itself.' The 'itself is' of desire is self-extending, the writing out of the ego and therefore 'not in itself desirable.' The manoeuvring of the key-word is artful in suggesting that desire can have a place within a pattern or in the approach to a pattern.[42] In contrast, the 'is itself' of love is the ultimate identity, totally self-inclusive, unmoving and undesiring, yet also the first and final cause of movement (the play on 'end' suggests consummation and extinction), the beginning and end of every circle that the turning of time inscribes. It is 'caught in the form of limitation' and that it is caught rather than held or chained as a previous image in the poem might suggest, is surely significant. 'Caught' suggests elusiveness, transience, the necessary vigilance of the seeker, and to some degree the complicity of the force sought. In more than one of these implications the poem returns us to the world of childhood, as that first illumination with which the initiation of its circle began and which is now 'caught' again in its closing images. The *Four Quartets* as a whole will find the same cause and end of movement within a proportionately larger form of limitation.

III

Burnt Norton inscribes a circle by ending where it began and suggests a circle of contraries in which the way up and the way down begin to approach each other. *East Coker*'s contraries are provided by the reversal in its opening and closing mottoes, with the yin and yang comprising the biological-teleological circumference, man's nature determined by his inheritance and his nature determined by his destiny. Alongside these circles runs the seasonal circle, moving through summer in the first section, late November in the second, and Easter in the fourth. These recurrences of a form should attract the reader's mind, but not enough to distract him from the onward movement which makes its way through them. *Burnt Norton*, as Helen Gardner observes, is a landlocked poem.[43] *East Coker* is set in a village not far from the sea. *Burnt Norton* contemplates its patterns of stability within the enclosure of a house. *East Coker*'s rhythms of erosion and turbulence proceed from the recognition that 'houses live and die.' Eliot's family lived in East Coker for two centuries before migrating to America. *The Dry Salvages* will re-enact that migration as a journey of the mind across the 'perilous flood' to those pillars of the known world that stand at the rim of formlessness. Meanwhile, the unavoidable need for migration must be established. The traditional 'In my beginning is my end' must be made to give way to the millennial 'In my end is my beginning.' The irrelevance of the past must force us into the future, if future and past are to be found in their final relationships.

The landscape of the poem foreshadows what is to come. The deep lane 'insists on the direction,' as the Quartets will until the shape of things is known. The light falls across an open field, leaving the lane shuttered with branches, suggesting not darkness at noon, but rather deep in the afternoon, the mind settled, slumberous, 'hypnotised,' 'absorbed, not refracted, by grey stone,' relinquishing that vigilance which is the price of its life. All that is left of the past is an open field, a loosened pane, a tattered arras, and a wainscot where a mouse trots, shaken by the wind which shook Gerontion's doorknob and which fifteen years after *East Coker* will blow into politics as the wind of change.[44]

The open field is not quite a *tabula rasa*. If we do not come too close to it, we can involve ourselves in what may be no more than a mirage. A weak pipe and a little drum declaim the music of tradition and degree. Dancing signifies matrimony and a concord made more distant because it is invoked in the archaic language of another Elyot who also lived in *East Coker*. And even as we imagine the remote presence of order, our attention is directed to its necessary decline. We are asked to contemplate not the dance but the feet of the dancers, which are 'earth feet' and 'loam feet' lifted in the clumsy mirth of those 'long since under earth.' As we slip down the chain of being from the commodious sacrament of matrimony into the coupling of man and woman 'and that of beasts,' from the stately rise and fall of houses to the rising and falling of the dancer's feet, the heavy rhythms stamp the past into an earth which is already 'flesh, fur and faeces' and so fitted to receive its new load of 'dung and death.' Dawn points but points at nothing. Another day gathers itself not for significance, but for heat and silence. The emptiness opens out in the stretched vowels of 'Out at sea the dawn wind,' then tenses and relaxes in the aimless animation of 'wrinkles and slides.'[45] The pointlessness which is being so carefully pointed at is carried further in 'I am here/Or there, or elsewhere,' with the 'here' at the end of the line registering a delusive certainty and the thought as it drifts over the line, dramatising the loss of location in space that matches the lack of contact with the past. It is enactment of the best kind, the rhythm matching the exact observation of the thing seen and both co-operating to delineate a state of being which the landscape particularizes. The fragment of the opening line which ends the section inherits and deepens this loss of place. Cut off from its completion, it is cut off from even location by its consequence. The beginning is not the start of a new advance, the point where the torch is handed on in the race of time. If houses rise and fall, so too do the accomplishments of one's poetic past. The beginning has to be nowhere, an open field facing the open sea.

The lyric of turbulence that begins section II is cast in the same octosyllabic measure as the lyric of order at the corresponding point in *Burnt Norton*. If the poet concludes that this way of putting it is not very satisfactory, it may be partly because the form-wrecking force of the destructive element cannot be adequately declared within so strict a containment. The suggestion is less than convincing. Indeed it can be argued that (as in section II of *The Dry Salvages*) elaborateness of design potentiates our awareness of anti-design or the absence of design. The truth is that the reader does not find the language of this lyric periphrastic or its conventions worn out until the author instructs him to be ruthless. The bleak self-scrutiny then involves the reader, reproaching him for his adhesion to the past, his own inability to make a wholly new start. But the 'worn out poetical fashion' is not simply in the poem to be identified and rejected. A main reason for its use is to invite the appropriate connections with the corresponding lyric in *Burnt Norton*. Echoes and affiliations chart the angry difference between a world distantly discerned from a formal garden and one hostilely confronting the experiencing self. The stars that once drifted now roll menacingly in 'constellated wars.' These wars transfer to the permanence of the heavens the 'long forgotten wars' once appeased by the trilling wire in the blood. The boarhound and the boar once reconciled in the approach to the still point, are now locked in hostility as 'scorpion fights against the sun.' The unison between macrocosm and microcosm is unison still, but a unison of destructiveness. Hollyhocks which aim too high tumble down in their violation of degree. Comets, themselves the sign of a disordered cosmos, weep in a manner uncharacteristic of comets. Leonids, which appear in mid-November three times every century, fly through the heavens in implied profusion. The hunt, previously limited to the boar hunt, now involves the heavens and the plains. Instead of a slowing down of motion as we ascend the ladder to the still point, we have an acceleration where all is whirled in a vortex. As the planets 'in evil mixture to disorder wander' we are reminded of Ulysses on degree,[46] the Elizabethan homilies, and other exercises in an out-of-date fashion. But to quote Ulysses again, the enterprise is not sick because degree is shaken. When we ask what the late November is doing with the disturbance of the spring, we recognize the transgression of decorum; but we should also remember that April is more than the cruellest month and that the elders of Canterbury should have done more than fear the disturbance of the quiet seasons.

The poetry does not matter, the poet says. It is a melancholy remark, but creative in its honesty. There are things that matter more than poetry and it is because of them that poetry matters. Language may be the instrument but it is also the consequence of the encounter of the self with the world. There are times when the solidified accomplishments of language seem only to inhibit the freedom and the force of that encounter. 'Peace in our time' was one form of a receipt for deceit, but politics is not the only seminary of illusions.[47] Because the poet's temptation is to live in his own past, to prolong rather than to move forward his accomplishment, it is necessary to be forced to begin again, to achieve the renewal of vision which is the renewal of language, to renounce autumn as the season of mellow fruitfulness and merited serenity. In the middle of the way Dante awoke to find himself in the dark wood and Milton, his light spent, 'Ere half my days, in this dark world and wide,' asked himself if his talent was not lodged uselessly with him.[48] This is the central and therefore the constant situation, surrounding us 'all the way' and not merely in the middle. Though Dante's voice is dominant, the dark wood also recalls *Comus* and it is in *Comus* that the traveller is menaced by monsters. 'Risking enchantment' recalls both the Lady's predicament and *Paradise Lost* I, 780-3. If enchantment is a peril, frenzy apparently is not. It is in fact the fear of yielding to abandonment, of recklessly making the commitment of blood shaking the heart, that constitutes the folly of age, masquerading as its restraint and wisdom. Yeats joins company with Eliot here.[49] His acre of grass matches Eliot's open field. An old house, with only a

mouse stirring in it, is common to both poems. Yeats's request that he be granted an old man's frenzy is reflected in
Eliot's dismissal of the fear of frenzy. The temptation is
'quiet' in both poems. The conclusion of both poems is that
old men should be explorers.

A place in poetry is not simply a location but a meaning.
In *East Coker* the previous emigration and the sea both for-
bidding and renewing act in co-operation with the reiterated
need for a new start. The lane 'dark in the afternoon' prefig-
ures Samson's anguished awareness of self-betrayal. It is an
awareness that applied strongly to the England of 1940 when
the responsibilities of self-scrutiny made it necessary to ask if
the strange gods that failed were the sole cause of failure.
With the houses under the sea, the past erased, and the future
unembodied, Samson's cry, and its entombing repetitions of
'Dark, dark, dark,' now explicitly initiate the procession into
nothingness. In commenting on the line and those that follow, Eliot judged 'interlunar' a 'stroke of genius' but added
that it was 'merely combined with "vacant" and "cave"
rather than giving and receiving life from them.'[50] This is a
reading which is less than sensitive and Eliot's adaptation of
the lines is not necessarily an improvement upon them.
Nevertheless, 'The vacant interstellar spaces, the vacant into
the vacant' does underline with sufficient wit the passion for
advancement in the galaxies of secular power. The repetitions
of 'vacant' also remind us that interstellar space is largely
emptiness and, as the vacant moves meritoriously into the
vacant, we can ask ourselves whether vacancy is not vacuity.
For Samson the sun and the moon were dark and (even more
painfully) silent. Eliot extinguishes in addition the lights of
lesser hierarchies that burn more brightly in the changing
world. It is the funeral that is silent. Reality cannot speak to
us (as it initially could not to Samson) because we cannot
recognize what must die. Nothing in fact has died and what
we have, even here, in typical Eliot fashion, is the ritual,
standing in for the reality. More images of darkness are added
in the effort of definition. A scene is being changed in a
theatre. An underground train is halted between stations. A
patient etherized upon a table is conscious, but conscious of

nothing. The common element in these images is an interim between two states, the pervading presence of nothingness, and the passive waiting for a transition which only outside forces can negotiate. Beneath these simulations we are led to the creative darkness, the voiding of the mind explored so strenuously in *Ash-Wednesday*, the stillness achieved so that one can be touched by the stillness. Not everything has vanished under the sea and the hill. The moments of illumination endure and they are 'Not lost, but requiring, pointing to the agony/Of death and birth.' The diminishing of the imperative force of 'requiring' by the less insistent 'pointing to' directs us to the Good Friday lyric which is to follow. It also suggests that the demand on us has been lessened and that the scene can change, the train move, and the act of surgery be completed because the agony has been borne by another. But the pointing is also to an example, to a road forward which we are called on to follow. All this has been said before by others as well as by Eliot. It will be said again. The capacity to say it restores a link with the past. A passage follows, saying it again, in a manner which the innocent have been known to find an example of Eliot at his worst. The words are actually those of St John of the Cross in *The Ascent of Mount Carmel* but the news calls for courage rather than the hasty revision of judgements. Considered purely as poetry, these lines are 'not very satisfactory.' Perhaps that is one of the reasons for quoting them. The poetry does not matter or, at least, ought not to matter, until there has been a change of scene in the theatre of the heart.

Poetical fashion is much in evidence in the lyric of section IV where the wry wit supports a tonality strikingly different from those offered by the corresponding lyrics in the other quartets. 'For the world, I count it not an inn, but an hospital; and a place not to live but to die in' is Sir Thomas Browne's improvement on Augustine[51] and Eliot elaborates on the improvement with a determination that is worthy of Cleveland.[52] But this is a poem of self-scrutiny, unlike *Burnt Norton*, which is a poem of impersonal speculation, or *The Dry Salvages*, which is a poem of public address. Self-scrutiny calls for the ironic scalpel and the questioning of the 'distem-

pered part.' The working out of the conceit is never less than
ingenious and external aids are not needed for us to discern
that the 'wounded surgeon' is Christ and the 'dying nurse' the
Church. The 'ruined millionaire' has been construed as God[53]
but a stronger case could be made out for Adam. The paradoxical proposition that we are restored by our sickness re-
affirms the familiar knowledge that the way down is the way
up and prepares us for the later understanding that meaning
can only be recovered by a deeper penetration into the hostility of experience. The lyric therefore has its place in the onward movement and, in charting the place, we can note how
the trilling wire in the blood is now a 'mortal' wire in which
'the fever sings.' The tenancy of the place, however, would be
dogged rather than spirited were it not for the oblique realism
by which the allegory is everywhere accompanied. Surgeons
are not always the embodiments of robust good health.
Nurses can sometimes give the impression of a constant endeavour 'not to please.' The 'absolute' or 'total' care that surrounds us in a hospital may seem designed to suffocate rather
than cure us. The diet in a hospital is frequently less than
varied and despite it (or possibly because of our ability to
absorb it) we find hope in Friday and in other days of the
week. In the hospital of our salvation the responses are more
complex. That we are 'sound substantial flesh and blood' is a
delusion. We can find Friday good because of the delusion.
We can also find it truly good because we have come to understand the nature of our fever.

The conclusion finds the poet in the middle which is the
beginning. The years *entre deux guerres* have been largely
wasted, as Milton wasted the years of the interregnum. We
can remember how the older poet, blind but undefeated,
made his 'wholly new start' and found the strength to give
himself to the writing of the most sustained and inclusive
long poem in the language. The purpose of a crisis is to break
open a horizon. Home is where one starts from and the statement inherits the sedulous lack of attachment by which the
last line of the first section was informed. The beginning is
made significant not by where it is or by how it has been connected but by the movement of departure from it. In this

particular cycle one is obliged to start when the imagination faces the outrage of the real, when the structures of thought and therefore of contentment which one had sought to establish must be laid open to the anger of experience. The poem seeks to prepare for this departure by returning to and reviewing its beginning, completing the circle with a final reversal that both encloses the poem and opens the way to an advance from its understandings. Thus the statement that the world becomes stranger and the pattern more complicated revalues the earlier discovery that the pattern is new in every moment, suggesting not the irrelevance of the past, but the need for a new venture to engage the new complexity. The pattern is, moreover, the pattern of 'dead and living.' In *Little Gidding* the dead will be the spokesmen not for what has been superseded, but for what remains undyingly alive. It is now not the intense, isolated moment that we seek, with the waste, sad time stretching before and after, but a lifetime burning in every moment, creative connection rather than timeless renewal. The cadences of the opening lines return, but in softer rhythms, that bind us less inexorably to the wheel. There is a time for youth with its evening under starlight, and for age with the photograph album of its memories. But there is also a time for exploration for which age may be qualified, since age is closer to the frontier. Here or there does not matter and the first implication is that the exploring impulse must be untramelled. But the line also takes up and redeems an earlier loss of orientation, already discussed. Here and now do not matter either. At first the line may seem to reconsider the 'Quick, here, now' which marks the illuminated moment in *Burnt Norton* and the risk of its passing unattended. But the modification is more probably to that nearly destructive sense of the uniqueness of the present which has characterized some of the more crucial findings in *East Coker*. The 'here or there' of place and the 'here and now' of time subtly relate love to exploration, while modulating the 'Love is itself' of *Burnt Norton* into the more attainable 'Love is most nearly itself.' The slowing down of the lines and their self-silencing, the achieved tranquility of 'cease to matter,' once again bring us to the edge of the stillness. Then, over Eliot's favourite double use of 'still,' the poem launches itself into its movement of exploration. The rising excitement of 'union' and 'communion,' the 'new intensity' in which the intense moment can be recaptured, are felt, but felt in relationship to the other side of the journey, 'the dark cold and the empty desolation.' The emptiness deepens, with the alliteration of 'wave,' 'wind,' and 'water,' the slight variation of 'vast,' the repetition of 'cry,' and the lighter alliteration of the petrel and the porpoise, seeming to reproduce the weightiness of the ground swell and the play of the surges that are mounted upon it. The threat is the promise and the end the beginning.

IV

The Dry Salvages opens in a tonality startlingly different from any previously encountered in the Quartets. The quality of that difference is sharply defined when we set the safeguarding 'I do not know much about gods' against the safeguarding 'perhaps' in the second line of *Burnt Norton*. This is the platform intonation instead of the Oxbridge voice, directed at the audience, not the object. It addresses us in a longer line, heavily freighted with anapaests and embodying what must by thought of by its owner as oratorical fullness. Stock formulations such as 'conveyor of commerce' and 'builder of bridges' exhibit a mechanical alliteration strikingly in contrast to the closing lines of *East Coker*. 'Worshippers of the machine' is a climactic effort at phrase-making in this manner, as is the empty ominousness of 'waiting, watching, waiting.' Parody offers itself as a muttered explanation, but to accept the offer is to relocate rather than to resolve the problem. A more likely beginning is the relationship between the popular and the poetic, with which Eliot has been concerned, particularly in his dramas. The commonplace originates in experience, but as words take the place of thoughts and feelings,[54] the commonplace becomes an evasion of experience. The river too can be tamed, its destructive energy civilized, and our responses to it then settle into stock responses. Our awareness of its seasons and rages becomes an acknowledgement rather than an encounter. In the end, even the speaker's warning that we ignore the river at our peril takes its place among the attitudes it seeks to reproach. 'I do not know much about gods' is a statement which the subsequent oration is designed to deny but which it ironically confirms. We will not know much about gods either until we are led back to the experience that once lay behind these verbal stereotypes. When the elemental achieves the renewal of language, the common word can be exact without vulgarity. It is a specification some distance from this opening exercise.

The movement into experience begins with the unpromising 'His rhythm was present in the nursery bedroom.' The 'rank ailanthus' of the next line is a phrase unexpected in its immediacy and as the world opens from the 'nursery bedroom' to the 'April dooryard,' we become aware of the blatancy and the expanding force of life, the rankness of the river in its many overflowings. The more discreet 'smell of grapes' civilizes the energy but also draws the world in around the autumn table. The final retraction is to the 'evening circle,' defensively close under artificial lights. The movement of growth and withdrawal is traced naturally by the momentum of the imagery. Modulating the lecturing voice, it indicates to us both that the voice is distant from the experience and that it was once connected to the experience.

When we have been made aware of the river as present in the rhythms and seasons of our lives, we can move back to the recognition that the river is within us. If, in contrast, the sea is all about us, that does not mean that the river is internal and the sea external. The changing, indefinite borderline, repeatedly penetrated, is finely drawn and redrawn by the verse. The effect is of two eruptive forces acting in concert, between which the outline of our identity seeks precariously to maintain itself. The delusive finality of 'granite' standing at the end of the line, as the cliffs stand resistant at the end of the land, is all but annulled by the penetrative force of the next line, the eroding momentum of 'reaches,' 'beaches,' and 'tosses,' with the final, repeated syllable tossed back and forth in the attacking spray. Left on the shore by the indifference of energy are 'hints of earlier and other creation.' The land on which these remnants are flung feels both the pressure of destruction and the presence of another life, alien because it is uncompromised, or in platform parlance, 'untamed.' These intimations have their long-term relevance since the climax of the poem will be the discovery of another dimension, transcendental rather than elemental. Meanwhile it can be noted that the sea also has its civilities. It can 'offer' its 'more delicate' forms of creativeness to our 'curiosity' in pools which assist the quiet of speculation. Having shown us its life it then reminds us of our death. The torn seine, the shattered lobster pot, and the broken oar bear witness to the sea's hostile energy. The gear of foreign dead men suggests the distance across which that energy can extend. Another country, of our own and not the sea's creation, is flung on our shores by this impersonal enmity. We turn again to the sea's penetrative force. This time the reach is further inland, with the salt on the briar rose and the fog in the fir tree. The sea has many voices but none are reassuring. The sea howl, the sea yelp, the whine in the rigging, the whistling of the groaner, the wailing warning from the headland, the sound of assault upon the granite teeth are threatening reminders of a life below consciousness by which consciousness is endangered. If it is ambivalently, both nourished and endangered, the poem's momentum so far is no encouragement to the apprehension of those creative relationships that make time the preserver as well as the destroyer. The 'menace and caress of wave that breaks on water' is potent in suggesting a withheld force with which we are able to live, only because it chooses to tolerate us.

The poem now takes up its recurrent consideration of time, setting apart the time rung by the unhurried ground swell from the time that we are able to compute or to experience. Some of the force of that ground swell is conveyed by the brief line with its closely packed stresses that is used to recognise it; and its distance from the time we know is widened by the separating force of the repeated 'older,' placed crucially at the beginning and end of the next line. The rhythms of human time are less potent and more agitated. The anxious worried women who count it can be those who, as in section IV, have seen their sons and husbands 'setting forth and not

returning' or those who, as in section V, 'fiddle with penta-
grams or barbituric acids.' Psychic time can be counted in
boredom or in fear. Those who unweave, unwind, and unravel
may be searching for a design, waiting for the inevitable, or
merely attempting to occupy an emptiness in which time
stops and time is never-ending. This is demonic timelessness,
the moment between midnight and dawn, redeemed in the
encounter in *Little Gidding*, in that uncertain hour before the
morning. The affinity with Penelope is persuasive but distant.[55] Ithaca is not threatened and nothing is postponed by
the unravelling and piecing together. We struggle to foresee
what can only be awaited. A higher voice must teach us to sit
still. The anxious rhythms subside and the ground swell returns, secure but inexorable. The bell clangs as it must for
every man, adding its soundings to the total of loss.

The first section of *The Dry Salvages* has moved us from
the stereotype to the reality which the stereotype once repre-
sented but from which it can now only distract us. The movement, like every advance of understanding, has been made
possible by and through a reconstituting of language.[56] It has
been apparent from the beginning that the earlier way of putting it was not very satisfactory; but the extent of evasion, of
the failure to respond beneath the crudities of acknowledgement, become apparent only as we enter the dark cold and
the empty desolation. The resources of language make possible the ancestral journey of the mind but it is a journey
back to the abyss of its origins. At the brink the mind must
verify that its creative structures are structures of self-realiza-
tion rather than devices of self-defence.

The second section begins in numbness. The silent withering of autumn flowers can be thought of as a reversed version
of the pathetic fallacy in which nature is treated not as human, but as denying itself the relief of being human. The
silent wailing, the motionless destitution, the wreckage inertly
drifting, are indications that the deception of the thrush has
led us to the unheard pain rather than the unheard music.
The bone on the beach – whiteness against whiteness – can be
contrasted with those other bones which were left for renewal
by the three white leopards. The bone's prayer, not yet de-

fined, is linked to an 'unprayable prayer' at an annunciation perceived, at this point, as calamitous. Are the prayers one, or confused into one, or are they to be contrasted? The questions are left open for the advance of understanding to resolve.

There are six stanzas in the second section. No line rhymes with any other in the same stanza but every line rhymes with its counterpart in every other stanza. The effect is consequently not that of regulated movement through a closed and containing entity but of a succession of open repetitions that are potentially infinitely extensible. The form is that of accumulation and the more its consequences are worked out, the more it is made to become through its further deployments an increasingly emphatic declaration of the meaningless. In addition, every line ends in an unstressed, or dangling syllable. The 'trailing/Consequence of further days and hours' is enacted in these hypermetric endings, nowhere more vividly than in the line just quoted, where the statement is one with its rhythmic mimesis. With the statement that 'There is no end but addition,' repeatedly endorsed by the stanza structure, what is achieved is the paradoxical marriage of elaborate form with the intense recognition of formlessness.

In the second stanza the numbness is internalized. The motionless becomes the emotionless. The wreckage is the wreckage not of lost causes, but of possibilities renounced. Yet to live among the ruins without complaint and with an appropriate capacity for self-denial does not result in any end but addition. Stoicism is not enough. That 'unattached devotion' which a public voice could conceivably call 'love of humanity' is also not quite sufficient. The final addition is a sum in defeat and as the suspended 'failing' of the third stanza attaches itself to pride (for which the secular name is 'self-respect'), and then to resentment at the betrayal of creative intentions by the failing body and the faltering intellect, we become aware that fame may not be the last of the noble mind's infirmities. The 'drifting boat with a slow leakage' is a modern version of a Renaissance image, Vittoria's soul 'like to a ship in a black storm.' With the proud full sails no longer part of the image, we can concentrate on the foundering in futility. The last annunciation answers the final addition. Its voice is now a clamour, undeniable as the boat drifts to the verge. One listens to it but does not necessarily respond to it. The prayer may still be unprayable.

It should not be difficult to find here the eloquent exploration of a crisis which Eliot's poetry has already passed through but which it is not exempt from passing through again. Before the thunder's message can be imparted, the mind must be made to realize that there can be no end but addition within its own perimeter. We cannot think of a time that is oceanless, or of an ocean that is not littered with wastage. Trapped by the metaphors of existence, we are conditioned to feel them as absolutes rather than metaphors. Indeed if we seek significance (or build our defences against the overwhelming futility) it is by rearrangement of the metaphorical material. We *have* to think of them as bailing, setting, and hauling, in endless prolongation which the rhymes between stanzas can endlessly support, rather than contemplate the termination of the process, and the totalling of the achievement, the 'haul which will not bear examination.'[57] Compulsive carrying-on may indeed be the mind's last refuge. It can be easier to extend the chain than to break it.

The last stanza returns to the beginning with intensifications. Flowers which have already withered continue to wither. To the dazed sensibility, pain becomes painless and motionless. Aimless continuance is made even more pervasive by the endless drifting of the sea itself. But the bone's prayer is now defined as a prayer to death. The annunciation, first calamitous and then undeniable, is now perceived as 'the one annunciation.' The unprayable prayer has become 'hardly, barely prayable.' These are small consolidations but at the margin inches are decisively significant. It is not outrageous and it may be part of the consistency of the life-act to say, notwithstanding the destructive weight of the evidence, that the past has another pattern and ceases to be a mere sequence.

It is not outrageous, but one is at least disconcerted by the lumbering wisdom of the interpreting voice, the dismissal of the 'popular' by a mind which at this point may be perilously close to the commonplace, and that climactic reference to a 'very good dinner' with its embarrassing alliance of levity and seriousness. After the preceding lyric with its anguished explorations, one might have expected the response to be more shapely. But poets fail and the failure matters less if it takes place before the final addition. As the disquisition proceeds to the relationship between experience and meaning, we find our way back to the familiar intertwining, the renegotiation of terms through spiralling repetitions that is so important a part of Eliot's poetic tactics. In this ascent we might note how the moment of happiness evolves (or is purified) into the 'sudden illumination' and how this in turn evolves into a meaning 'beyond any meaning/We can assign to happiness.'[58] The 'beyond' does not necessarily point to ecstacy. The poem here is reconsidering the fifth section of *East Coker*, first by its reference to 'another pattern' rather than to a pattern growing more complicated, and now in the introductory 'I have said before,' with its explicit pointing to a previous understanding. Tradition is alive in the illuminated moment, a tradition going back to 'old stones that cannot be deciphered.' But the truth of experience, the limits which the meaning must accommodate, are not solely in the historical record. The documents of the past define the civilizing effort, reassuring us about its nature and its future. The backward look can be deliberate, reviewing the adequacy of the definition. Or it can be the half-look over the shoulder, making of history a continuing flight from our origins. To move beyond 'happiness' is to move into inclusiveness, to accommodate within the containment of meaning the contrary yet complementary propulsions in man's nature. *East Coker* had pointed to an agony 'requiring death and birth' and *The Dry Salvages*, moving through that death, has reached the conclusion that the 'moments of agony' have the same permanence as the moments of happiness. Time moves through the co-presence of these moments and so time is indivisibly both destroyer and preserver. The evocation may well be of the dance of Shiva in which creation and destruction inseparably manifest the play of energy in the theatre of time.

We stand in a poem which is still a work of the night and so it is the destructive potential which is dominant in the images. The river with its 'cargo of dead negroes, cows and chicken coops' requires us to remind ourselves of its other possibilities as a conveyor of commerce. The 'bitter apple and the bite in the apple' suggest original sin doubled before it is redeemed. The 'ragged rock in the restless waters' conveys erosion by alliteration. It is a seamark in navigable weather but what it always was is destructively revealed in the sombre season and the sudden fury. Yet the Church too is most fully itself and present most creatively in a season of adversity. In each case we can draw the creative parallel or find the creative complementarity. But we do so in resistance to the pressure of the images, a resistance which is our own evocation of the nature of the life-act. Chaos when we confront it must be registered as overwhelming. But in recording the evidence we record our awareness that the evidence is not final.

The application of what Krishna meant might be clearer if we knew the precise context in which he meant it and the antecedent of the pointing 'that.' The somewhat ornate imagery which follows does not recall the *Gita* though it may be meant as a graceful acknowledgement of the decorum of Oriental poetry. On the other hand, the withering before the blooming does suggest that the way forward is the way back and the lack of penetration in the imagery is adequately evaded in 'We cannot face it steadily.' That time, unlike the wounded surgeon, is no healer is a proposition to be seen in engagement with time as destroyer-preserver. The crucial consideration is perhaps not the nature of time, but how we act in time. Yet action cannot be undertaken in the time-flow by referencing it to a self which moves through that flow and which is discovered to be constant and to stand apart from that movement. The self changes as much as the river into which it steps and the images of journeying which occur in section III of each quartet are used here to suggest that every journey is an act of changing. Whether we stand at an apex (the liner's wake), or look back to an apex (the rails narrowing behind the train), both we and our placing of our point of departure are continuously moving in time-experience. If the world and the experiencing self both change, both must be referenced to a point beyond change for a valid geometry of action to be constructed. The voice in the rigging (to be contrasted with the whine in the rigging) which 'descants' to us, but not into the ear which is the shell of time, or in language which moves 'only in time,' provides an intimation of this point. 'Descant,' incidentally, is a term ingeniously chosen if we accept it as signifying a melody or counterpoint written above the theme which it accompanies. The voice is heard by the mind only when 'time is withdrawn' and when the mind is adequately disengaged from past and future, action and inaction. Right action, disinterestedly undertaken, is similarly free from precedent and consequence, from what a previous poem apprehended as the protective enchainment of past and future. Its essential character can only be discerned if we cease to judge it in relation to its fruits. Since life moves and creates within a train of cause and consequence, action *sub specie aeternitatis* must be thought of in the shadow of the finality of death and the presence of death must be found in every moment.

These understandings have scriptural roots as well as roots in the *Gita*.[59] The history of the mind repeats itself and the form of repetition is to be sought even in the rhythms of the individual history. At this point, the meeting of East and West subsumes a previous meeting which was even then described as not accidental. Some critics seem to believe that wisdom is not served by having this meeting take place, that the uniqueness of Christian revelation is not to be associated with inferior or approximate understandings. Religious humanism is the term which might be used by the sanctified to describe this betrayal. Eliot himself has encouraged such critics by affirming that the difference between those who accept and those who deny Christian revelation is 'the most profound difference possible between human beings.'[60] The imagination displays more charity, making one wonder again whether it is not the true instrument of knowing. A critic cannot be obliged to accommodate his response to the full width of the poem though if he does not, it is not the poem that will be impoverished. If the accommodation is made, we will find ourselves asked to attend to more than a concurrence of understanding, or an advance upon a previous effort

at synthesis. The *Gita* is a sermon on a battlefield, the purpose of which is to make right action possible in a crisis of
choice. The education of the mind for action involves nothing less than a complete exposition of the relationships between time, reality, and the self. It is so in *Paradise Lost*, first
in the two angelic tutorials that comprise Adam's formal education, and then in the reader's enlightenment, by Adam's
education both formal and experiential, comprised within the
larger effects of the poem. It is so again in *Four Quartets*, the
crucial difference being that the shaping relationships are not
expounded, but built and tested by the exploring consciousness. Nevertheless, the necessary universe has the same dimensions and it is the size and reach of the context that is significant. We can now appreciate the restraint shown in *Four
Quartets*, the advance from concepts into experience, the
sounding and survival of the darkness, before terms such as
'meaning' and 'action' are permitted to join the poem's philosophical vocabulary.

The Lady's shrine stands on the promontory, the intercessive force reaching into the sea, as the sea in the first section
reached into the land. The prayer to her takes a line from St
Bernard's prayer to the Virgin in *Paradiso* XXXIII. For those
who go down to the sea in ships, the time of death is indeed
every moment and the Lady's prayers are invoked for those
who are bereaved as well as for those who lie in the sea's lips,
the sea's throat, or deeper still within that destructive ana-
tomy. The allusion to Jonah seems clear and Matthew 12:40
is probably attracted. We can also think of the mind as held
by the darkness in its journey of understanding, a darkness
which will not reject it until a higher principle comes to its
aid.

Communication with Mars and conversation with spirits
are even more popular today than when Eliot wrote *The Dry
Salvages*. The spirits differ from the voice in the rigging and
one can report the behaviour of the sea monster in ways
which have little to do with Jonah and Christ. The parodic
catalogue enumerates the palliatives to which we turn when,
as in Luke 21, there is 'distress of nations, with perplexity.'
Man's curiosity searches past and future and the word 'curio-

sity' is accurate, though unpalatable. A search for knowledge, an enlargement of the field of investigation, is more respectable than a search for nostrums; but the two are not wholly removed from each other, as is apparent from the Faustian bargain. We are brought back to a familiar Eliot understanding, the inability of the mind to escape from itself or to find the roots of significance within its boundaries. It can extend its activities but it cannot transcend them. In the end it is trivialized by its unavoidable clinging to its own dimension.

Parody here may be the prelude to a deeper misapprehension but the tone of the summing up does not suggest that a refinement of parody is in the making. A failure of language might be a better explanation if one were necessary. But it is not evident that the language fails. We might note how the point of intersection is dramatized by placing one 'dimension' at the end of a line and the other co-ordinate at the beginning of the next. Going back, we might observe how a similar positioning is used to distance apprehension from what it seeks to apprehend. Moving forward, we can find the same device shaping our awareness of the unattended moment. The use of a repeated positioning tactic to achieve subtly and designedly different effects does suggest that a poetic intelligence remains in control with the degree of cohesiveness that is called for in a decisive effort at articulation. Responding further, we can note how 'occupation' (not 'calling' or 'vocation') relates itself to the time-consuming exercises of man's time-bound activity, exemplified in the parodic catalogue. Othello's occupation is more dignified but the use of the word is intended to call for its abandonment, to suggest through its inadequacy the nature of the unitive commitment. As 'occupation' is superseded, the 'something given' which takes its place looks forward to the 'gift, half-understood.' The location strengthens our consciousness of the donation; the response comes from another dimension which we cannot reach up to, but which must reach down to us. 'Taken' in the next line completes the compact, but we are made conscious of the cost of taking, of a 'lifetime's death in love,' even as we balance against the cost, the vital expansion of 'time' into 'lifetime.' This is the proper end of the understanding that the time of death is every moment. The next line is fervent in its repose-fulness, suggesting through its prolongation by the repeated vowels, and by the quietening force of its sibilants, the extension of its own stasis, the continuing death in love that is necessary if the terms of life are to remain apprehended. It is an effort so far beyond the ordinary pursuit of the meaning-ful that we can move back with relief (but with a corrective awareness of what is compromised) to the definition of the more common pursuit. The 'unattended' moments of illumination are now characterized, the characterization remaining carefully general. It is not the particularities of the context that matter but that which it suddenly, yet evidently contains, the world beyond it which it is made to manifest. These are only hints and guesses, the reflecting voice concludes, only to take the phrase back, replacing it by 'hints followed by guesses.' The mind is not overwhelmed by illumination. It remains active, following up the hint (more than one scientific hypothesis is the result of educated guessing), modifying earlier and inadequate formulations, reconsidering its thoughts in the process of thinking. In the end the hint will be only half-guessed and the gift only half-understood. The climax of the effort of understanding, shaped and reshaped, intermittent and tentative, moving forward through its own inadequacy, is such knowledge as we can have of Incarnation.

In the seventh of the choruses to *The Rock* Eliot elaborates on the nature of the point of intersection. The concept had therefore been in his mind for some years. It is withheld from the vocabulary of the poem, just as 'meaning' and 'action' had been previously withheld, until the poem was ready to receive them. The understandings that the poem attains or approaches would lose their propriety if they did not relate themselves to the poem's outreaching effort and were, in some degree, the consequence of that effort. The Incarnation is a climactic understanding justified not as dogma, but as dogma standing at the horizon of experience, entering into a deeply creative relationship with the search for meaning that has found its way to the threshold.

Nothing in the language so far suggests a failure of apprehension, or misconceived apprehension, unless successful apprehension means that the other-than-Christian reader should find himself disqualified. The climactic understanding, it is true, is not set apart from the understandings that have led to it, so that any man whose mind has been invaded by the presence of the real can continue to participate in the advance of the poem. To many, this openness will not be calamitous. As for the didactic import, we can concede that 'Prayer, observance, discipline, thought and action' is not a particularly exhilarating formula even though action comes rousingly at the end of the sequence. The point is that epiphanies are not enough, that for the consolidation of insight we must take the measures which collective wisdom has found to be reliable. Less than encouraging also is the news that the 'impossible union of spheres of existence' is a theoretical ideal for 'most of us' and that we are undefeated only 'because we have gone on trying.' But the thought proceeds from *East Coker*'s 'For us there is only the trying/The rest is not our business,' making it difficult to argue, as Hugh Kenner wittily does, that the passage is Matthew Arnold's road out of *East Coker.*[62] We can regret, if we wish, that the character-building perseverance recommended suggests that right action largely consists of playing the game in the right spirit. A determined source hunter might remember Bruce and the spider. Perhaps it is more profitable to recognize that the question which Eliot is facing, and which he was not to answer to his satisfaction until *The Cocktail Party*, is whether there can be a way that leads to meaning between the sterile death-in-life of the waste land and the consuming life-in-death of the saint. The response to the question has to begin in an acute consciousness of the distance between the saint's way and what is possible for 'most of us.' But poets, it should be added, are not indisposed to irony and it is not unusual for a poet to warn us that what he is about to do cannot be done. *Little Gidding* will proceed to make real the impossible union of spheres of existence. What has been achieved is an approach to the meaning. What remains is a restoration of the experience.

If we decline to be overcome by the discouraging dourness, we can see that the last line of *The Dry Salvages* points to a life of 'significant soil,' not too far from the yew tree with its double affirmation. The temporal reversion which nourishes this life has a firm place among the concerns of poetry. 'Love's mysteries in soules doe grow/But yet the body is his booke' is Donne's classic statement of the relationship, a statement turning on his deft use of the proposition that nature is one of the books of God.[63] Yeats can descend from the steep ascent to Byzantium to embark not reluctantly but exultantly on that 'dolphin-torn, that gong-tormented sea' which is the proper element of poetry. Even more pertinent are Milton's quiet closes, with their varied stylings of the return. 'Nothing can be reckoned as a cause of our happiness which does not somehow take into account both that everlasting life and our ordinary life here on earth.'[64] This is Milton's finding as a university student, a finding which the course of his poetry consistently documents. Eliot too knows that our responsibility is to ordain wisely and to act rightly in this world of good and evil in which we are placed. The purpose of the act of poetry is not to escape from this responsibility, but to surround it and to enable it to move forward.

V

The detail of the pattern may be movement, but there is a pattern of movement that needs to be distinguished, at least initially, from the pattern which stands apart from but is declared by the movement. If we were to draw a graph of the poem's becoming, one way of drawing it might be to say that *Burnt Norton* is concerned with constructing concepts, *East Coker* and *The Dry Salvages* with the application of those concepts to a widening and increasingly destructive area of experience, and *Little Gidding* with the transfiguration of the facts within the area by the finality of a truth which lies beyond it.[65] In abstracting from the poem to this degree, we should note that several crucial additions to the poem's terminology – the point of intersection, Incarnation, and right action – are introduced only after an approach has been made to the meaning. A nicety of this reticence is the withholding of the key concept of meaning itself. Moreover, when the concept becomes accessible it is as the result of a reaction rather than a continuing advance. It arises when we recognise the ground of our being as the need for significance and when we confront the defeat of experience, its final failure to render itself significant. At that point it becomes not simply possible but an essential dimension of the act of life for it to find a connection to another pattern. In a poem of the exploring and the out-reaching consciousness the connection can be stated in doctrinal terms at the periphery of understanding; but within the poem it must be known by its effects, seen not as it is but as it appears intermittently 'in a watery mirror.' The Incarnation is mentioned only once, approached through studiously distant approximations. The 'impossible union/Of spheres of existence' must be found thereafter in what the poetry does.

Little Gidding expands the moment in and out of time to a season 'not in time's convenant.' Midwinter spring, pole versus tropic, frost versus fire, windless cold that is nevertheless the heart's heat, the blinding glare of the ice versus the glow of understanding in the mind, indicate the tensions that surround and enter suspension. The life-giving response to the timelessness shares the same sense of detachment into the real, with the dumb spirit stirring, the soul's sap quivering between melting and freezing, and the hedgerow blanched with snow, transforming *East Coker*'s 'late roses filled with early snow' into a flowering 'not in the scheme of generation.' The immediacy of the real, its strange but compelling presence in phenomena, is a fit entry into a poem in which transformation must be achieved through summation.

Since the moment is timeless it is independent of any approach to it. It is the same at the end of the journey, whatever the route, wherever one starts, irrespective of the season, whether one comes at night, broken and on the way to death, or comes by day, not knowing what one has come for, facing that blindness in the early afternoon which picks up and transforms *East Coker*'s 'dark in the afternoon.' The purpose is altered in fulfillment just as the pattern was new in every moment, but the recognition now suggests, not that we cannot step twice into the same river, but that rivers while following unexpected courses all flow eventually into the same sea. There can be other places penetrated by timelessness: Iona at the 'sea jaws' associated with St Columba, the 'dark lake' of Glendalough associated with St Kevin, the desert of the Thebaid associated with St Anthony, and the city of Padua associated with the other Anthony.[66] This particular poem and this particular journey approach the meaning as it turns behind the pigsty to the dull façade and the tombstone. Though Robert Adams criticizes Eliot's inability to convey 'a sacramental view of the world, a rich dwelling in the holy joy of ordinary things,'[67] few poems would have the courage to introduce and the capacity to survive such details at a point of understanding which is clearly felt as exalted. On the other hand, 'You are here to kneel/Where prayer has been valid' and the subsequent listing of what fails to be prayer strike a note which is unfortunately to be heard elsewhere. Since *Little Gidding* is a poem widely and justly admired it may be time to point out that much of it would be unacceptable without the validating force of the other three Quartets behind it. It may be a merit of the poem that it is so solidly Anglican property, but the suspension of disbelief also has to be meaningful for those whose approach to the place is from other places. Phrases like 'England and nowhere. Never and always' do not encourage this suspension.

Death is the subject of the second section, recited comprehensively as the death of the elements. Eliot has recognised but has refrained from confirming the view that each of the Quartets assumes 'some relation to one of the four elements and the four seasons.'[68] In fact the 'death of air' involves references not only as one might expect to *Burnt Norton*, but also to *East Coker* and even to that 'deceitful face of hope and despair' that is seen down the stairway in *Ash-Wednesday*. The death of earth involves both 'dead water' and 'dead sand'; and the death of water is presented jointly with the death of fire. It is therefore not easy to attach each stanza, or for that matter each element, to one of the Quartets. We can concentrate instead on the vanities that are dismissed and the negligences that are avenged: the burnt roses of desire and memory, the house of a man's rootedness, the toil of cultivation, the town that is now ranked in significance with the weed, the sacrifice that is denied and the sanctuary that is forgotten. The ravaging force thus moves from personal attachments to the civilizing effort and finally to the sacred places that our own 'marring' has exposed to its destructiveness. The verse declaring that force also moves from the transitory and limited residue of 'dust on an old man's sleeve,' through the exhausted contention of laughter 'without mirth,' to the more menacing mockery of the sacrifice derided.

The bitterest mockery is the defeat of the self, the bodily decrepitude that does not lead to wisdom, the ironic crown that is placed on a lifetime's effort. The encounter scene that the lyric of the second section prefaces has been commented upon earlier in this book, but there are other linkages that need to be made. We might note, for example, how the setting 'Between two worlds become much like each other' and 'Between three districts where the smoke arose' remembers both the 'impossible union of spheres of existence' in *The Dry Salvages* and the 'place of twilight where three dreams cross' in *Ash-Wednesday*. Yet the disclosures made at this 'intersection time' do not initially advise us that 'all manner of thing shall be well.' Indeed the 'bitter tastelessness of shadow fruit' is a line strongly evocative of the metamorphosis of Satan and his angels and therefore places in the most mocking of perspectives the exercises in futility which follow. The end of the affair has not been reached with that 'cold friction of expiring sense' which is the profit of Gerontion's 'chilled delirium.' There is 'conscious impotence,' lacerating laughter at what ceases to amuse (recalling the laughter of the death of earth), rending re-enactment, and the helpless addition of wrong to wrong in the chain of self-imprisonment. A synopsis such as this is needed to convey the weight of frustration that is registered. It would be an exaggeration to say that the poetry annuls this weight but it does succeed in not being overcome by its own lucidity of aftersight and foresight. The strange meeting at a point of disengagement between last year's words set down in last year's language and next year's words awaiting another voice, sets the bleakness of our situation dispassionately before us, as well as the 'discipline thought and action' which remain the only way to amend that bleakness.

The *Gita* has much to say on non-attachment and Eliot may have been remembering and commenting on Krishna's counsel in describing the three conditions that look alike and flourish in the same hedgerow. We can infer that the conditions co-exist in the mind and that of the three only indifference is 'unflowering,' as the earlier poetry has so insistently taught us. Attachment is not thought of as a chain to be severed, a falsifying relationship to be shed or renounced, but rather as a form of life that is capable of leading to the higher life of detachment. If we remember *Burnt Norton*'s characterization of the relationship of love and desire we can think of memory as a force of liberation, assisting the expansion of love beyond desire. Love of a country too begins in a local attachment that remains in being however much it may be diminished in importance, as the area of commitment is enlarged. History, which is a form of collective memory, similarly assists the expansion and liberation of consciousness. In relating that consciousness to what will later be called 'a pattern of timeless moments' it relates it to the unmoving and the eternally present without uprooting it from the world of time. As a chain of events, history may be servitude. As a structure of significances, it can put before us the nature of our freedom. Even Eliot's tactics of literary allusion can profitably be treated as suggesting how history is testimony.

Sin is behovely and even small quarrels have their place in the grand design. There is playfulness in the verse here, beginning with the not very inspired borrowing from *Hamlet*, proceeding through the punning use of 'genius,' and elevating to the status of 'strife' the dissensions in the Little Gidding community. The strife is more serious and the pattern beyond partisanship more remote when we think of King Charles visiting Little Gidding at nightfall, of Charles, Laud, and Strafford on the scaffold, of those, including Crashaw, who died forgotten in exile, and of their opponent, Milton, who died not violently or forgotten, but 'blind and quiet' in his own isolation. If memory is to be used for liberation, rather than for the strengthening of attachments into fixations, we should refrain, in thinking on these figures, from sounding the alarm by ringing the bell backwards, from following an antique drum, or from summoning the spectre of a rose. The spectral rose may be from Browne[69] but we can take it to stand for an attachment judged as nostalgic, whereas the true rose is the symbolization of pattern and energy in their ultimate detachment. Reviving old politics may seem an unreal issue to have raised in an England then being ravaged by Nazi bombers. 'Who but Eliot,' Graham Martin asks, 'would be likely to have felt drawn away from the contemporary crisis by the "antique drum" of Charles the Martyr's confrontation with Oliver Cromwell?'[70] That is a way of putting it but it should be remembered that the contemporary crisis is brought before us in section II and in the apocalyptic lyric of section IV. Moreover, a philosophic poem largely concerned with time must at some point consider the uses of history. The past does not liberate us when it merely entrenches us in our allegiances; we might, for example, be better critics if we did not insist on believing that the maladies of literature began with the dissociation of sensibility. If the past is to enter a creative relationship with the present it can do so only by helping to define a timelessness that is shared by past and present. It is not a question of who was right – that discrimination is silenced by the use of 'fortunate' and 'defeated' – but of why there should be moments of agony. Every contemporary crisis asks that question. The past liberates us when it helps to suggest that a response to the question is not impossible.

In the end the response is apocalyptic. All shall be well but none of us can escape the cost of having it made well. *The Dry Salvages* had concluded that the moments of agony were as permanent as the moments of happiness and that the meaning we approached had to comprehend the co-presence of those moments. In *Little Gidding* the serenity of the revelation to Dame Julian of Norwich[71] stands side by side with the terror of the descent of the dove. The tongues which tell us of meaning are always tongues of flame, whether in 'the communication of the dead,' the declaration of the 'one refuge from sin and error,' or the composition of the 'crowned knot of fire.' Even the dove's demonic counterpart, the 'dark dove with the flickering tongue,' provides a place of desolation for an unearthly meeting between a man of letters and his 'history.' The creativeness of fire is thus insistently part of the new fire sermon and it is largely because of this insistence that the poem is able to sustain an accommodation of the moments of agony. The love that devises the torment appears in a manifestation sharply different from the unmoving mover of *Burnt Norton*, the moment of heightened serenity in *East Coker* when 'here and now cease to matter,' and the 'life-time's death in love' in *The Dry Salvages* which is the Saint's being rather than his 'occupation.' Later, the new manifesta-tion will be seen more tranquilly in 'the drawing of this Love and the voice of this Calling.' The interpenetrations of the poems keep in relationship the many faces of the 'unfamiliar name.'

The sharp change from the lyric to the discursive (or as Donald Davie would have it from Mallarmé to Cranmer)[72] that is so characteristic of the Quartets takes place again at the opening of section v. At this point it is a neat flourish on the proposition that 'to make an end is to make a beginning.' 'The end is where we start from' leads the proposition back to *East Coker*'s 'Home is where we start from.' As the poem returns home, with every word now at home, the joint truth of both propositions is carried forward in the poetic act. If last year's words belong to last year's language every poem is an epitaph or, to put it slightly less bleakly, a symbol per-fected in death. It becomes part of the eloquence of history. It is also a milestone in the way forward which is the way back, a step to the block and the fire (remembering *Little Gidding*), to the sea's throat (remembering *The Dry Salvages*), or to an illegible stone (remembering *East Coker*'s 'old stones that cannot be deciphered'). The poem's own history as we return through it can be seen as a pattern of timeless mo-ments and as we enter a secluded chapel 'while the light fails' (remembering *Burnt Norton*'s 'draughty church at smoke-fall'), the history of the effort to comprehend irradiates the recognition that 'History is now and England.'

We shall not cease from exploration. The garden is at the frontier, the 'last of earth,' as well as the 'source of the long-est river,' the climax of the interior journey. Even now the hidden waterfall and the children in the apple tree are not known but 'heard, half-heard in the stillness.' The poetic intelligence is fastidiously at work in the 'half-heard' which is audible against a stillness which it points at rather than violates, and in the repetition which strengthens the fragile intimation. The advance upon that unheard music with which the poem's journey began is deliberately minute and therefore intensely meaningful. We are also kept aware of a stillness caught in time and so heard between two waves of a sea which remains the element of our voyaging, as well as potentially the sea of our peace into which the individual rivers of our wills flow. As the circle closes, a line from *Burnt Norton* is quoted in its entirety.[73] That which is here and now, yet always, which is ultimate and yet in the quick of the moment, is now defined as a condition of complete simplicity, recalling Yeats's 'simplicity of fire.'[74] The cost of that simplicity is 'not less than everything,' the purging of the dross of all distractions. It is a cost of which the poem has made us aware, particularly in its final lyric. The Dantean remembrance already mentioned now appropriately precedes the gathering of the ever-changing flames into the safeguarded cohesion of the crowned knot and the final union of the fire with the rose.

CHAPTER SIX

The Detail and the Pattern

As the œuvre is put together and as the energies running through it are intertwined in the finality of the crowned knot, we have to ask ourselves how the achievement is to be valued. The fiftieth anniversary of *The Waste Land* was a natural occasion for stock-taking and the opinions offered do not suggest that a final addition is in sight, or even that Eliot's work has established a clear and accepted relationship with the ideal order of the past. Even the character of that work, the degree of its cohesiveness, still seems open to dispute. Robert M. Adams declares for instance 'that a linear view of Eliot simply will not work – he was not given to developing in consecutive patterns at all.'[1] It is possible that 'linear' is not the best word to characterize, in achievement or deficiency, the journey of the work and its forces of questioning and settlement. The patterns of the work, moreover, are probably patterns because they are more than consecutive. But even if we allow for refinements of terminology, a view is being offered by Professor Adams which this book has consistently sought to resist. If the resistance has been successful our sense of the work will need to be formed around an opposing assumption.

Another way of viewing *The Waste Land* is to regard it as a crucial or even consummating stage in the self-declaration of the modern consciousness. Walton Litz may have this possibility in mind when he suggests that it might be best 'if we refrained at least for a little while, from thinking of *The Waste Land* as a major revelation of man's spiritual plight ... and thought of it instead as a master document of the modernist movement in literature.'[2] Professor Litz's subsequent list of subjects to which the aspiring Eliot scholar might give his attention suggests that we should approach *The Waste Land* mainly as a primer of modernist tactics; and as a primer it has merits which are distinctive and unrepeatable. But tactics are eventually only justified by what they succeed in bringing into being. Eliot would almost certainly have rejected the view that what came into being was 'a major revelation of man's spiritual plight' and we are persuaded to do likewise, both by that probability and by the colouring of the phrase; but we can scarcely admit the contrary view that the poem does no more than place in shifting relationships a heap of fragmentary perceptions, displaced understandings, and brilliantly broken images. *The Waste Land* is a deeply representative poem in more than the narrow sense of being accepted as a sacred text (or textbook) of the twenties. Its achievement is to delineate within the particularities of literary history a state of being that is far more than the state of the moment. It is a state that has been passed through before and will be passed through again. But to pass through it in a way that speaks to other men it is necessary to set it down in the idiom of contemporaneity. Eliot does so in a language act of unique capability, an effort of definition which because of its scrupulousness is a potential extrication from what has been defined. The act of language once accomplished is left behind and is not repeated. The poem is an epitaph in this sense but also in the sense that it brings to its most brilliant and telling application a set of tactics especially representative of a particular moment in literary history. Stylistically, *The Waste Land* is a period piece and this could be fatal with a lesser poem. It is not fatal with *The Waste Land* because the accuracies of Eliot's language are not merely historically representative but also lead us to the knowing and comprehensive naming of a place which the mind must live through in its movement of self-renewal.

The nature of that movement is suggested by Robert Langbaum when he observes that 'The Waste Land dramatizes the making of an identity' and that 'the Quest is for personal order that leads to cultural order and cultural order that leads to personal order.' Once this is seen 'the poem turns out more positive than we think it.'[3] Better terms might be chosen than 'culture' and 'identity' to define the dialectic of exploration, though any terms chosen must be used with the recognition that it is the purpose of a poem of engagement to discover through that engagement the entities engaged. With these reservations it can be said that the mind falls slightly short of making or finding itself in its movement through the Waste Land. Rather it is advised, and even then ambiguously and at its horizon, of those principles, not as yet meaningful, on which it can proceed to make itself. This is progress of a kind and both The Waste Land and The Hollow Men (which Professor Langbaum does not find 'positive')[4] are affirmative in the sense that they do not make affirmation impossible. To measure this seemingly negligible advance and to grasp its crucial significance, it is necessary to place The Waste Land in the continuity of Eliot's poetry. We then become better aware of the complex and protracted process by which the self in its continuing engagement with the world is able to reoccupy its own lost reality, to know and to make itself, and to reconstitute the world in that self-making. Learning is exploration and knowledge is both discovery and recovery. These propositions become all the more meaningful when the loss of Eden itself is established as a principle by the exiled and exploring consciousness. To discard the rites of illusion and destruction and to reach understandings which are truly creative, not as organizational statements, but as vital principles which the œuvre attains and embodies, is to make evident who, in the twentieth century, is the true heir of the poetry of experience.

The poem of self-achieving has an extensive history and we can take it back at least as far as Lycidas, which even more than *Alastor* is a root poem of the modern consciousness. Eliot's accomplishment is an œuvre of self-achieving in which every major poem negotiates the right of the next poem to exist. Moreover, while the poems are consecutive (though not without the retreats and evasions which accompany the reality of any advance), each poem treats itself as a wholly new start, realizing itself in a new act of language. *Four Quartets* stands as the culmination and re-enactment of this movement. As M.H. Abrams remarks, the poem is 'a remarkably inventive rerendering of the genre and *topoi* of the poet's circuitous journey through his remembered past.' Its 'evolving meditations play complex variations upon the design and motifs of the poet's educational progress.' The conspicuous difference is 'that Eliot's version of the Romantic genre of the artist's self-formative progress is also a reversion to its Christian prototype, the Augustinian *peregrinatio vitae.*'[5] This book is in evident agreement with Professor Abrams's view and the possibility that Eliot may indeed be the substantial heir of the romantics has an ironic relish that we need not decline to savour. But we should add that Donne and his colleagues were excited by circular journeys and that 'self-formative progress' is a conspicuous feature of *Paradise Regained* and *Samson Agonistes*, not to mention *Paradise Lost* and *Lycidas*. Eliot's innovativeness, however, does not simply lie in a conflation of the Augustinian and the Romantic for which Milton and his age provided some seminal anticipations. What distinguishes this particular circular journey is the magnitude of its preface, which can be said to occupy the entire œuvre, up to and including *Ash-Wednesday*. A circle of exploration cannot be meaningful until a point of departure can be established, more stable that 'here/Or there, or elsewhere' which registers not a point of origin, but the 'drifting boat' of the self, in its necessary severance from origins. The need for a preface of this magnitude becomes more evident when we remind ourselves of the nature of the exiled consciousness. If that consciousness is sufficiently deep in alienation, it will demonstrate its removal from the source by compulsively preferring its own rites of indifference, survival, conservation, and apparent renewal to the obliterating pro-

spect of dying into life. The preface which is the self-educa-
tion of this consciousness must move through and discard the
false possibilities and must earn its connection with the
source it has all but erased. It will find its way to the threshold of the garden because the experience, if fully confronted
and resolutely persisted in, will prove self-forming to this degree. But the garden must be found in order to be lost and
the 'remembered past' of which Professor Abrams speaks is
also the history which the œuvre has succeeded in building.
The end is where we start from and the spiral of process is to
the circle of design, as becoming is to being and the movement to the pattern. But the poem is able to inscribe these
relationships only because a previous end has been established
as a beginning.

When George Orwell, in looking at *Four Quartets*, com-
plains that 'something has departed, some kind of current has
been switched off, the later work does not *contain* the earlier,'[6] he is protesting against the lack of a consistency such as
this book has been endeavouring to demonstrate. The conclusion that Eliot 'does not really *feel* his faith but merely assents
to it for complex reasons' and that his faith 'does not in itself
give him any fresh literary impulse'[7] is not unexpected, given
the extent of direct statement and the explicit attachments
of the poetry after *The Hollow Men*. The real question is not
whether a faith has led to a literary impulse but whether a
literary impulse, or more correctly an endeavour of the whole
mind in evolving acts of literature, has called for a faith in the
final stage of its growth and self-formation. Some who would
accept this formulation nevertheless feel that Eliot fails to
comply with it. C.K. Stead in allowing a chapter of his influential book to be entitled 'The Imposed Structure of *Four
Quartets*'[8] is clearly advising us of a failure in the poetry.
John W. Aldridge in a recent review finds the early work
'grounded in the emotional specifics of experiences closely
observed and deeply felt' and the later work 'abstract, conceptual, and didactically theological.' Eliot, he concludes un-
kindly, 'in effect gave up being a poet in order to become
secure in the universe.'[9] Richard Wollheim similarly argues
that 'Eliot, in the pursuit of a certain kind of security or reas-

surance that we are in no position to define, was progressively led to substitute, in his mind, on the one hand, ideas of less content for ideas of more content, and, on the other hand, poorer or softer ideas for better and stronger ideas.'[10] Robert Adams explicitly endorses this conclusion.[11] It is not clear that ideas, whether soft or hard, play any important part in Eliot's earlier poetry. But Professor Wollheim is presumably pointing to a lack of toughness in the later work, a too great readiness to accept the peace of dogma, instead of continuing the sceptical and poetic struggle. If so it would seem helpful to confront this conclusion with that reached by F.R. Leavis in his consideration of Eliot's later poetry. Leavis finds the poetry 'essentially a work of radical analysis and revision, endlessly insistent in its care not to confuse the frame with the living reality, and heroic in its refusal to accept.'[12] It should be apparent where the balance of this book lies. We can conceivably differ in our weighing of the evidence, but we should seek to be guided by the evidence itself, in its interpenetrations and in the full range of its complexity, rather than by prepossessions which question the right of a poet to conceptual apprehension, or his right to entertain the strange gods of a theology.

It has been suggested that Eliot's poems compose a continuity, but that the continuity is negotiated in acts of language which differ from each other according to the stage they make real in the forward and circling movement. The most respectable of the objections to *Four Quartets* are those which are based on the alleged disjunctions of language in the poem. For Donald Davie, the distance between the poem's two languages approaches the distance between Mallarmé and Cranmer.[13] Since the antithesis is presumably intended to shock the reader into a perception of the problem, it may be less than helpful to search the poem for traces of Cranmer's presence. Mallarmé's presence may seem a different matter and is attested to by at least two 'borrowings.' But the lyrics most likely to manifest this presence range from the metaphysical to the apocalyptic and their design upon us is probably no less palpable than that of the poetry (or the prose) of statement. On the other side, the discursive passages can be drily poetic, particularly when the sparse resources, the lack of imagery, and the tightly controlled effort at definition compound what Yeats called 'The fascination of what's difficult.'[14] At their best these passages instruct us in the meaning of *logopeia*, 'the dance of the intellect among words.'[15] In their midst an image such as 'The loud lament of the disconsolate Chimera' can surprise us with its resonating loneliness, or the final lines of *East Coker* can sound both the apprehension and the excitement of life in the bare statement that 'Old men ought to be explorers.' It becomes difficult to see the Quartets as built on an uneasy relationship between the poetry of evocation and the prose of statement. We should be thinking in any case not of statement, but of the stabilization of thought, its *arrival* at a point where a formal proposition can express its balance. The language can fail to meet this requirement but it fails for reasons which have little to do with the extent of assertion in it.

For C.K. Stead, 'the English poetic tradition has always occupied middle ground between pure discourse and pure image.' The Quartets represent a dignified but not wholly successful attempt to achieve a tenancy of this middle ground. Stead does not argue that the 'didactic' passages necessarily fail. The second voice (that of the poet addressing his audience) can remain that of a man 'whose intellect we admire and whose ideas we have learned to approach at least with the caution of a bomb-disposal unit.' But the intellect can meddle with the lyrical (as in *East Coker* IV) and the second voice can retreat from prose to pontification. The 'uneasy alliance of discourse and image' gains strength throughout the Quartets but is constantly bedevilled by a disavowal of the physical world and the consequent disjunction between image and idea.[16]

There should be no question that Eliot seeks a middle ground, that he is concerned with poetry both as a lonely, uncompromised act of definition and as an act of speech that is eloquent to other men. The dialect of the tribe is purified by insight; but those insights in turn are given substance by their entry into the dialect. Among the many progressions which can be charted in *Four Quartets* is the movement from the personal to the public, from the enclosed garden to the historic community. Parallel to this movement is the reconciliation of the poetic with the commonplace, of the lyric with the meditative and discursive, of the moments of insight with the institutions of understanding, of doctrine with the experience that seeks it and finally forms a creative relationship with it. Not all these consorts can be made to dance perfectly together, but Eliot strives for the right interplay between them with craftsmanship, commitment, and intelligence. Given the parallel and converging lines of movement, the evolution in recurrence on which the form insists, it seems more than normally unhelpful to isolate passages of discourse from the Quartets and then to castigate them for their 'prosiness.' Eliot learned his craft in a school of which one cardinal principle was that 'poetry must be as *well written as prose.*'[17] There is inferior prose in *Four Quartets* but much of the prose shows us the mind in the act of finding, or provides us with *la peinture de la pensée*, to quote Maurice Croll's description of one kind of baroque style.[18] Pound, who said that poetry should be impassioned prose, also said that 'all poetic language is the language of exploration.'[19] In any case we should not, in reading *Four Quartets*, attend to the surface alone. The decisive complexities in a long poem are likely to be those of reverberation rather than surface. A poem of sufficient magnitude writes its history and its progress is a citation and fulfillment of that history. Finally, a poem which seeks a living relationship between intuition and discourse is not merely situating itself on a prudent middle ground but attempting to establish the wholeness of the mind in the necessary modes of its activity. *Four Quartets* would be a poor thing if it were only its 'lectures'; but it would not be much better if it were no more than its lyrics.

Stead's second objection remains to be considered. That the soul should divest itself of the love of created things can be a necessary preliminary to its achieving detachment. It does not follow that the divesting must be permanent. The love can be restored, but restored in right relationship to a higher commitment which was lost in the lower distractions. In the totality of Eliot's poetry, little is said about this restoration. Helen Gardner has observed that Donne was a person in whom the appetite for life was crossed by a deep distaste for it.[20] Eliot's work conveys nearly all of the distaste and hardly any of the appetite. The city of God may be the only real city but a talent nourished exclusively by this insistence will find itself in the desert, rejecting that lament of the disconsolate chimera which is the sign of the human rather than the half-heard music. In the end the anguished awareness of discontinuity, of the severance of being from becoming, must be superseded by the conviction of continuity, of being celebrated in becoming. There is evidence that Eliot was moving in this direction, despite his long involvement with the poetry of distaste. *The Dry Salvages* contemplates a temporal reversion to a life of significant soil. *Little Gidding* documents that reversion with a generosity of commitment to the world of time, not previously found in Eliot's poetry. In *The Family Reunion*, Harry calls to Mary in language that anticipates the moments of illumination in the Quartets. Yet Mary's voice, though joined with the 'distant waterfall,' is heard as one hears 'the moderate usual noises/In the grass and leaves, of life persisting/Which ordinarily pass unnoticed.'[21] In *The Cocktail Party*, Reilly puts to Celia the choice between the way of the saint and the way of reconcilement 'to the human condition.' Both ways 'avoid the final desolation/Of solitude in the phantasmal world.' When Celia asks if the ordinary way is the best life, Reilly replies

It is a good life. Though you will not know how good
Till you come to the end. But you will want nothing else.
And the other life will be only like a book
You have read once and lost. In a world of lunacy
Violence, stupidity, greed ... it is a good life.[22]

Some might wish for a more energetic return to what Denis Donoghue calls the ordinary universe, but the temperate realism has its rightness and is in harmony with the sounds 'of life persisting.' Moreover, every man's work must be allowed the form of limitation that is the source of some of its strength. For Eliot, the peril has always been that we condemn ourselves to the worst by not seeking the best. It is a choice of either the vision or the desolation. Commitment to the vision may result in a scorn of the desolation that can be anti-poetic. Acceptance of the desolation can mean a refusal of the search for meaning which is the basis of the poetic effort. In this most fundamental of dilemmas, *Four Quartets* represents the finding of a middle ground. It is the fulfillment of a long endeavour that keeps the shape of that endeavour in balance, so that the weight of futility does not overwhelm our final understanding of what can be heard in the 'moderate usual noises.' We begin with discontinuity, a deep sense of the cleavage between vision and desolation. We end with a tentative continuity, the impossible union of spheres of existence, made real in the poetic enterprise. The poem which Eliot writes between these points is a poem which tells us that self-renewal is endless and that in this rented house we do not reach conclusion once we discover the nature of our tenancy. Through the persistence of its hunger for meaning it attains eligibility for its own forward movement. Achieving the longed-for turn from chaos to design, it nevertheless continues to fare forward, recapitulating and reopening its history in a further circle of recurrence and reversal. It is both a meditative poem of the mind and a heroic poem of the human journey, brought into being with a depth of craftsmanship that can originate only in a resolute openness to experience. For that craftsmanship Pound sets down the exacting standard: 'The poet's job is to *define* and yet again define till the detail of surface is in accord with the root of justice.'[23] Eliot has defined and redefined, making the detail not only consistent with the root but the main means of discovering what the root is.

Notes

CHAPTER ONE

1 'Tradition and the Individual Talent,' *Selected Essays* (London 1934) 21

2 'John Ford,' *Selected Essays* 21

3 *The Spectator* CXLVIII (1932) 360-1

4 'W.B. Yeats,' *On Poetry and Poets* (London 1957) 252-62

5 'What is Minor Poetry,' *On Poetry and Poets* 49-50

6 'George Herbert' in *British Writers and Their Work No. 4*, ed. J.W. Robinson (Lincoln 1964) 63. Writing in 1949 on Joyce, Eliot similarly observes that 'Joyce's writings form a whole,' that 'as with Shakespeare, his later work must be understood through the earlier and the first through the last,' and that 'it is the whole journey, not any one stage of it, that assures him his place among the great.' Quoted in John D. Margolis, *T.S. Eliot's Intellectual Development 1922-1939* (Chicago 1972) preface x-xi

7 For a fuller development of this view, see B. Rajan, *The Lofty Rhyme* (London 1970).

8 For a fuller development of this view, see B. Rajan, *W.B. Yeats: A Critical Introduction* (London 1965). An important early

statement is made by Hugh Kenner in *Gnomon* (New York 1958) 9-29.

9 'Lancelot Andrewes,' *Selected Essays* 340

10 *The Letters of Ezra Pound*, ed. D.D. Paige (New York 1950) 171

11 *After Strange Gods* (London 1934) 40

12 *The Letters of Ezra Pound* 171

13 This passage is examined in more detail on pp 27-8 and pp 111-12

14 *Essays Ancient and Modern* (London 1936) 150-1

CHAPTER TWO

1 W.B. Yeats, *Collected Poems* (New York) 232, 244, 196

2 *To Criticize the Critic* (London 1965) 125-6. Cp. 22

3 *Ibid.* 130

4 *Ibid.* 129. See also 'The Waste Land: Paris 1922,' *Eliot in his Time*, ed. A. Walton Litz (Princeton 1973) 75

5 *The Waste Land: A Facsimile and Transcript of the Original Draft*, ed. Valerie Eliot (London 1971) 100-1; *Ara Vus* [sic] *Prec* (The Ovid Press, London 1920); 'Al Som de L'Escalina,' *Commerce* (Autumn 1929); 'Ash Wednesday IV,' *Collected Poems* (New York 1962) 90; *The Waste Land*, line 428

6 *To Criticize the Critic* 22-3

7 *On Poetry and Poets* (London 1957) 31

8 Samuel Johnson, 'John Milton,' *Lives of the English Poets* (London 1925) 1, 112

9 See in particular *Facsimile* 4-5, 54-9.

10 *Facsimile* 54-69, 128n

11 'Ulysses, Order and Myth,' *The Dial* LXXV (5 November 1923) 483

12 *Facsimile* 10-11. Pound's objections to the original epigraph from Conrad (*Facsimile* 125n) led to the epigraph we know, Conrad being remembered in the epigraph to 'The Hollow Men.'

13 The correct reference is v.2.

14 *Facsimile* 80-1, 88-9. The error persists in the Boni and Liveright text (*Facsimile* 146).

15 *Facsimile* 70-1

16 *Facsimile* 76-9

17 Yeats, 'Lapis Lazuli,' *Collected Poems* (London 1950) 292

18 *Facsimile* 79

19 *Ash-Wednesday, Collected Poems* 88

20 F.R. Leavis and Q.D. Leavis, *Lectures in America* (London 1969) 55. See also *Education in Our Time and the University* (London 1969). On the unity of Eliot's accomplishment, see also Northrop Frye, *T.S. Eliot* (Edinburgh 1963) 49 and Leonard Unger, *T.S. Eliot: Moments and Patterns* (Minneapolis 1967) 31-5.

21 'A Babylonish Dialect,' *T.S. Eliot: The Man and his Work*, ed. Allen Tate (London 1967) 243. The movement from *The Waste Land* to *Four Quartets* is perhaps not best described as the movement from image to idea. It could be better – though not altogether adequately – described as the movement from an enabling experience to a subsequent experience that bestows meanings on the previous experience. We should also note that if, as D.W. Harding points out (*Experience into Words*, London 1963, 106), *Burnt Norton* is characterized by its creation of concepts, the movement of the Quartets then is from concepts, through experience, to an order built upon and looking back on both.

CHAPTER THREE

1 Grover Smith, *T.S. Eliot's Poetry and Plays* (Chicago 1956) 39; George Williamson, *A Reader's Guide to T.S. Eliot* (London 1955) 90; D.E.S. Maxwell, *The Poetry of T.S. Eliot* (London 1952) 95-6

2 Nevill Coghill, 'Sweeney Agonistes,' *T.S. Eliot: A Symposium*, ed. Richard March and Tambimuttu (London 1948) 82-7

3 T.S. Eliot, *The Use of Poetry and the Use of Criticism* (London 1933) 106

4 Harold F. Brooks, 'Between *The Waste Land* and the First Ariel Poems: *The Hollow Men*,' *English* XVI 93 (1966) 89-93. Closer to the view adopted in this chapter is D.E.S. Maxwell's finding (*The Poetry of T.S. Eliot* 137) that the beginnings of faith can be seen 'in "The Hollow Men," often looked on as the nadir of Eliot's despair.'

5 The term was coined by Coleridge. See Eliot, *The Idea of a Christian Society* (London 1939) 35; Roger Kojecky, *T.S. Eliot's Social Criticism* (London 1971) ch. 1.

6 *The Letters of Ezra Pound*, ed. D.D. Paige (New York 1950) 169-71

7 Russell Kirk, *Eliot and His Age* (New York 1971) 76-7
8 W.B. Yeats, 'Meru,' *Collected Poems* (London 1961) 333
9 Grover Smith 102; Williamson 161
10 *Essays Ancient and Modern* (London 1936) 67
11 'London Letter,' *The Dial* 71 (1921) 214, 217
12 *The Use of Poetry and the Use of Criticism* 106
13 *Essays Ancient and Modern* 159
14 Yeats, 'The Magi,' *Collected Poems* 141
15 'Lancelot Andrewes,' *Selected Essays* (London 1934) 340
16 Eliot, *The Use of Poetry* 148; Grover Smith 123
17 Luke 2:25-35
18 *Selected Essays* 259-60
19 Yeats, *Collected Poems* 244, 266
20 Philip R. Headings, *T.S. Eliot* (New Haven 1964) ch. 2
21 Grover Smith 313n
22 Grover Smith 130
23 An important unpublished comment by Eliot on the recognition scene in *Pericles* is quoted by Elizabeth Drew, *T.S. Eliot: The Design of his Poetry* (London 1950) 159.
24 *Facsimile* 57, 65

CHAPTER FOUR

1 E.E. Duncan Jones, 'Ash Wednesday,' *T.S. Eliot: A Study of His Work by Several Hands*, ed. B. Rajan (London 1947) 38-9
2 F.R. Leavis, *English Literature in Our Time and the University* (London 1969) 118-22
3 Edmund Wilson, *Axel's Castle* (New York 1943) 130
4 Yeats, 'Upon a House Shaken by the Land Agitation,' *Collected Poems* 106
5 Grover Smith 144
6 See Russell Kirk 175, for varying interpretations of the three white leopards.
7 Headings 77-8
8 *The Letters of W.B. Yeats*, ed. Allan Wade (New York 1955) 343
9 Leonard Unger, *T.S. Eliot: Moments and Patterns* (Minneapolis 1967) 50-1. An even more exotic borrowing suggested by Professor Unger is from the article on cannibalism in Hastings's *Encyclopaedia of Religion and Ethics*.

10 Headings, from whom several of these details are taken, provides the best available account of links between Dante and
Eliot.

11 Grover Smith 148

12 'Baudelaire in Our Time,' *Essays Ancient and Modern* 73-4

13 *Selected Essays* 377

14 Grover Smith (p 151) suggests that the processional image has
less in common with Dante than with the progress of Lucifera
in *The Faerie Queen.*

15 Duncan Jones 52

16 Max Eastman, *The Literary Mind* (New York 1935) 111

17 'Milton 1,' *On Poetry and Poets* (London 1957) 143

18 The many religious and literary evocations of the desert-
garden symbolism are discriminated by Northrop Frye,
T.S. Eliot (Edinburgh 1963) 63-5.

19 Donne, 'A Hymn to God, My God in My Sickness'; Joseph E.
Duncan, *Milton's Earthly Paradise* (Minneapolis 1972) 211

20 Helen Gardner [ed.] *John Donne: The Divine Poems*
(Oxford 1952) Appendix F

21 Williamson (pp 207-8) notes the resemblance between the
imagery here and the images Eliot associates with Massachu-
setts in his 'preface' to Edgar Ansel Mowrer's *This American
World.* Eliot's use of the New England landscape is examined
by D.E.S. Maxwell (pp 144-6), who argues that 'the emphasis
which his [Eliot's] descriptions lay on the harsh and tenacious,
expose the Puritan feeling that man's attainment of spiritual
peace, as much as his creation of earthly beauty, must depend
on his own power to struggle against circumstance.'

22 Duncan Jones 56; Unger 68. Headings (pp 73-5) provides an
account of the relationship between the language of *Ash-
Wednesday* and that of the Ash Wednesday services of the
Anglican *Book of Common Prayer.*

23 *Paradise Lost* XI: 349-54

CHAPTER FIVE

1 'Ulysses, Order and Myth,' *The Dial* LXXV (Nov. 1923) 483

2 Grover Smith 162

3 Maxwell (pp 131-2) finds this description 'strongly reminiscent
of Heine's adulatory account of his seeing Napoleon march by.'

4 Aristophanes' *The Knights* compares a politician to a sausage seller.

5 Edmund Husserl, *Ideas*, trans. W.R.B. Gibson (London 1931) 127

6 F.O. Matthiessen, *The Achievement of T.S. Eliot* (New York 1959) 82-3

7 'Poetry by T.S. Eliot,' *University of Chicago Round Table* (No. 659) 10. Quoted in Grover Smith 159

8 Aristophanes is again in the background. Williamson (p 199) notes that the frogs foretell storms in *Georgics* 1.

9 Stephen Spender, *Poems* (London 1933) 56, 69

10 C. Day Lewis, 'The Magnetic Mountain,' *Poems 1929-33* (London 1938)

11 *Choruses from 'The Rock'* 11

12 C. Day Lewis, *Poems* 150

13 Grover Smith 251, 320n; Robert Sencourt, *T.S. Eliot: A Memoir* (New York 1971) 197, 253n

14 *New York Times Book Review*, 29 November 1953. Reprinted in *T.S. Eliot: Four Quartets*, ed. Bernard Bergonzi (London 1969) 24. Despite Eliot's suggestion that *Burnt Norton* originated in leftover lines from *Murder in the Cathedral*, it is *The Family Reunion*, published after *Burnt Norton*, to which the poem attaches itself most strongly. See Helen Gardner, '*Four Quartets:* A Commentary' in *T.S. Eliot: A Study of His Work by Several Hands*, ed. B. Rajan (London 1947) 52-3; Hugh Kenner, *The Invisible Poet* (London 1960) 258-61; Leonard Unger, *Moments and Patterns* 82-6; Louis L. Martz, *The Poem of the Mind* (New York 1969) 109-14.

15 *The Invisible Poet* 127-9

16 D.W. Harding in *Scrutiny* 1936. Reprinted in *Experience into Words*

17 '*Four Quartets:* A Commentary' 58-60

18 C.K. Stead, *The New Poetic* (Harmondsworth 1967) 170-7

19 *The Invisible Poet* ch. VI; Denis Donoghue, *The Ordinary Universe* (London 1968) 240-6. These accounts should be supplemented by that of Northrop Frye, *T.S. Eliot* 77-9.

20 Kenner 256

21 Stead 171-2; Kenner 262; Kirk 295, 300, 306

22 See *T.S. Eliot: A Study by Several Hands* 80. Some of the treatments of time and pattern in the Quartets are considered by Bodelsen, *T.S. Eliot's 'Four Quartets'* (Copenhagen 1966) 35-7.

23 See Kenner 251.

24 In his commentary on J. and R. Maritain's *Situation de la Poésie* (*New English Weekly*, 27 April 1939), Eliot observes that emotions themselves are constantly being lost and that they must be 'always rediscovered.' The poet's occupation is both 'the endless battle to regain civilization in the midst of continuous outer and inner chaos' and 'the struggle to conquer the absolutely new.'

25 *Notes Towards a Supreme Fiction* (Cummington 1942) 18

26 Yeats, 'Upon a House Shaken by the Land Agitation,' *Collected Poems* 106

27 Kenner 266-71. According to Kenner (p 163) it is in *The Hollow Men* that Eliot 'first ventures on the structural principle of all his later work, the articulation of moral states which to an external observer are indistinguishable from one another, but which in their interior dynamics parody one another.'

28 The trend was initiated by Donald Davie's 'T.S. Eliot: The End of an Era' (reprinted in *T.S. Eliot: 'Four Quartets,'* ed. Bernard Bergonzi). Russell Kirk can now say (p 300) that critics 'almost to a man' assign *The Dry Salvages* 'a dignity of style well below that of the other Quartets; some of its lines are perilously close to prose.'

29 Helen Gardner in her edition of *The Elegies and the Songs and Sonnets of John Donne* (Oxford 1965, p 184n) describes the debate between the old and new optics as 'unsettled at the Renaissance.' Donne employs the old optics in 'The Ecstacy' and Milton makes use of them as late as *Samson Agonistes* (83, 163).

30 A variety of literary links are suggested for what might be called the rose-garden experience. See in particular Helen Gardner 62; Louis L. Martz, *The Poem of the Mind* 109-14.

31 The lotus is mentioned here for the first and only time in Eliot's poetry. Its relationship with the rose, the circle, and

the still point, as affirmations of the mandala pattern, are discussed by Elizabeth Drew (*T.S. Eliot: The Design of His Poetry* 175-8).

32 According to Morris Weitz ('Time as a Mode of Salvation'; reprinted in *T.S. Eliot: 'Four Quartets,'* ed. Bernard Bergonzi 138-52), Eliot's theory of time is neo-Platonic rather than Heraclitean or Bergsonian. But the neo-Platonism is post-Augustinian. Martz (pp 114-15) makes an important suggestion to this effect. For a fuller examination see C.A. Patrides, 'The Renascence of the Renaissance: T.S. Eliot and the Pattern of Time,' *Michigan Quarterly Review* XII (1973) 172-96.

33 Grover Smith 257

34 Joseph Chiari, *T.S. Eliot: Poet and Dramatist* (London 1972) 88; Grover Smith 257; Harry Blamires, *Word Unheard* (London 1969) 16. See also Philip Wheelwright, 'Eliot's Philosophical Themes,' *T.S. Eliot: A Study by Several Hands* 100-1. In *The Use of Poetry and the Use of Criticism* (p 147), Eliot quotes Chapman on the 'burning axletree' and admits that the image has 'some personal saturation value' for himself. See also 'Seneca in Elizabethan Translation,' *Selected Essays* 74.

35 Kenner 254

36 'The "Pensées" of Pascal,' *Essays Ancient and Modern* 151

37 *Paradise Lost* VIII: 452-9

38 The *Bhagavad-Gita* ch. 11, in *A Source Book in Indian Philosophy*, ed. S. Radhakrishnan and Charles A. Moore (Princeton 1957)

39 Kenner 256-7; Chiari, *T.S. Eliot: Poet and Dramatist* 90

40 Grover Smith 260; Blamires, *Word Unheard* 28-9

41 Grover Smith 261; Headings 124-5; Blamires 33-4. Unger (p 81) is among the critics who associate the kingfisher with the Fisher King.

42 The possibility is taken up in *Little Gidding* III where memory brings about the 'expanding/Of love beyond desire' and thus liberates us 'From the future as well as the past.'

43 Helen Gardner 62

44 The 'silent motto' on the arras is according to Elizabeth Drew *tace et fac* ('Be silent and act'). It is one more rendering of the relation between stillness and motion.

45 Northrop Frye (p 34) finds an echo from Tennyson in the word 'wrinkles.'

46 *Troilus and Cressida* I.iii. 75-137

47 Eliot records that he was 'deeply shaken' by the Munich crisis and that the events of that month brought home to him and to others 'a profounder realization of a general plight' demanding 'an act of personal contrition, of humility, repentance and amendment.' The month threw in doubt 'the validity of a civilization.' *The Idea of a Christian Society* 63-4

48 Milton *Sonnet* XIX

49 Yeats, 'An Acre of Grass,' *Collected Poems* 346-7

50 *On Poetry and Poets* 141

51 Thomas Browne, 'Religio Medici,' II ii; *The Prose of Sir Thomas Browne*, ed. Norman Endicott (New York 1967) 83

52 The current adverse estimate of the lyric (See *T.S. Eliot: 'Four Quartets'* 18-19) is not entirely shared by the appraisal which follows.

53 Blamires 68

54 *Choruses from 'The Rock'* IX. This chorus is particularly relevant to the passages on language in the Quartets.

55 Blamires 90

56 Hugh Kenner, whose affection for *The Dry Salvages* is not excessive, considers 'the twenty-three-line sentence' that enumerates the sea's voices the 'most powerfully articulated passage' Eliot has ever published (p 269).

57 It is notable that the bailing setting and hauling continue while 'the North East lowers/Over shallow banks unchanging and erosionless.' Mutability is avoided so that futility can be made permanent.

58 In a conversation between St John Perse and Einstein (quoted by Kirk 142n) Einstein, in recognising the affinity between poetic and scientific insight, characterizes the 'mechanics of discovery' as 'neither logical nor intellectual' but as 'a sudden illumination, almost a rapture.'

59 Eliot's first allusion to the *Gita* is in five unpublished lines (*Facsimile* 110-11) beginning with 'I am the Resurrection and the Life' and ending with a reference to the *Gita* IX 16 (*ed. cit.*).

In *The Dry Salvages* II 47; III 30 and VIII 5, 6 are among the verses remembered.

60 *Revelation*, ed. John Baillie and Hugh Martin (London 1937) 1-2

61 F.R. Leavis in his comments on this passage (*Education and the University*, London 1943, pp 102-3) sees the crucial affirmation as seeming 'to strain forward out of the poem' and demanding 'to be referred back to what has gone before.' The poem's explorations are conducted with penetration and stamina 'below the conceptual currency; into the life that must be the *raison d'être* of any frame – while there is life at all.'

62 Kenner 271

63 'The Ecstacy,' *The Elegies and the Songs and Sonnets of John Donne*, ed. Helen Gardner 61

64 'Seventh Prolusion,' *Complete Prose Works* I (New Haven 1953) 291

65 See ch. 11, n21.

66 Kenner 272; Bodelson 105n

67 Robert M. Adams, 'Precipitating Eliot,' *Eliot in His Time*, ed. A. Walton Litz (Princeton 1973) 150

68 Bodelsen 32, quoting a note by John Hayward to Pierre Leyris's French translation of the Quartets

69 Grover Smith 289. See Frye 88. Yeats's attempt to summon the spectre of a rose is recounted in *Autobiographies* (London 1956) 181.

70 Introduction to *Eliot in Perspective*, ed. Graham Martin (London 1970) 19

71 Helen Gardner 75-6

72 Donald Davie, 'Anglican Eliot,' *Eliot in His Time* 195

73 The quotation not only completes the circle but underlines the transfiguration of 'the bird and roses of *Burnt Norton* into the dove of *Little Gidding* and the rose of fire and light at the end of that poem; that is, nature becomes a symbol of a spiritual truth which transcends it.' Elizabeth Drew, *T.S. Eliot: The Design of His Poetry* 187-8.

74 'Vacillation' *Collected Poems* 285. See also 'Byzantium' 280-1.

CHAPTER SIX

1 Robert M. Adams in *Eliot in His Time*, ed. Walton Litz 151

2 Litz '*The Waste Land:* Fifty Years After,' *Eliot in His Time* 8

3 Robert Langbaum, 'New Modes of Characterization in *The Waste Land*,' Litz 119

4 Robert Langbaum, *The Poetry of Experience* (New York 1963) 94

5 Meyer H. Abrams, *Natural Supernaturalism* (New York 1971) 319-21

6 George Orwell, review in *Poetry London* 1942; reprinted in *T.S. Eliot: 'Four Quartets,'* ed. Bernard Bergonzi 81

7 Orwell 86

8 In *T.S. Eliot: 'Four Quartets'* 197-211

9 *The Saturday Review* 9 March 1974, p 27

10 'Eliot and F.H. Bradley: An Account,' *Eliot in Perspective* 190

11 Adams, Litz 148

12 *Education and the University* 103

13 Davie, Litz 195

14 Yeats, *Collected Poems* 104

15 'How to Read or Why,' *Literary Essays of Ezra Pound* (London 1954) 25

16 C.K. Stead, *The New Poetic* 177-84

17 *The Letters of Ezra Pound* 48

18 Morris W. Croll, *'Attic' and 'Baroque' Prose Style*, ed. J. Max Patrick, Robert O. Evans, and John W. Wallace (Princeton 1969) 210. In 'From Poe to Valéry,' *To Criticize the Critic* (London 1965) 40, Eliot quotes the following remark from Valéry: 'In my opinion the most authentic philosophy is not in the objects of reflection so much as in the very act of thought and its manipulation.' The observation points to the modern literature of self-consciousness, the self-reviewing poem of the poetic act. Nevertheless, the most potent dramatization of 'the act of finding' remains the ascent of the hill of truth in Donne's third satire.

19 *Ezra Pound: A Critical Anthology*, ed. J.P. Sullivan (Harmondsworth 1970) 53

20 Introduction to *John Donne: The Divine Poems* (Oxford 1952) xxxv

21 *The Family Reunion* (London 1939) 59
22 *The Cocktail Party* (London 1950) 123-4
23 *The Letters of Ezra Pound* 277

Index

Abrams, M.H. 130-1, 147n
Adams, Robert 121, 127, 132, 147n
Aldridge, John W. 131
Andrewes, Lancelot 11, 48, 65-6
Aquinas, Thomas 90
Aristophanes 142n
Arnold, Matthew 17, 47, 118
Auden, W.H. 48, 77
Augustine, St 25, 103, 130

Baudelaire 22, 46, 63
Bergson, Henri 144n
Bernard, St 115
Bhagavad Gita, the 26, 94, 113, 114-15, 123, 145-6n
Bible, the: Ecclesiastes 59, 80; Ezekiel 59; Jonah, 115; Kings 59; Luke 49, 115; Matthew 115; Micah 66

Blamires, Harry 91, 95, 144n, 145n
Bodelsen, Carl 143n, 146
Bonagiunta de Lucca 58, 61
Brihadarayanaka Upanishad 31-3
Brooks, Harold F. 40, 139n
Browne, Sir Thomas 56, 103, 124, 145n
Buddha 25, 88
Burne-Jones, Sir Edward 62

Cavalcanti, Guido 57
Chapman, George 91
Charles I, 123, 124
Chiari, Joseph 91, 144n
Cleveland, John 103
Coghill, Nevill 39, 139n
Coleridge, Samuel Taylor 139n
Conan Doyle, Sir Arthur 51